TORN TOGAS

TORN TOGAS

*The Dark Side of
Campus Greek Life*

ESTHER WRIGHT

Fairview Press   *Minneapolis*

Published by Fairview Press, 2450 Riverside Avenue South, Minneapolis, MN 55454.

Library of Congress Cataloging-in-Publication Data

Wright, Esther, 1969–
    Torn Togas : The dark side of campus greek life / Esther Wright.
        p.   cm.
    Includes bibliographical references.
    ISBN 0-925190-94-2 : $19.95
        1. Greek letter societies—United States. 2. College students—United
States—Conduct of life. 3. n-us. I. Title.
LJ51.W75 1996
378.1'98'55—dc20   96–13371
                                                                 CIP

First Printing: July 1996

Printed in the United States of America
00 99 98 97 96   7 6 5 4 3 2 1

Jacket design: Circus Design

Publisher's Note: Fairview Press publishes books and other materials related to the subjects of social and family issues. Its publications, including *Torn Togas,* do not necessarily reflect the philosophy of Fairview Hospital and Healthcare Services or their treatment programs.

For a free current catalog of Fairview Press titles, please call this toll-free number: 1-800-544-8207.

To my precious daughter, Alexandra—
I pray you experience a better world

ΠΔΣΩΠΔΣΩΠΔΣΩΠΔΣΩΠΔΣΩΠΔΣ

CONTENTS

ΠΔΣΩΠΔΣΩΠΔΣΩΠΔΣΩΠΔΣΩΠΔΣ

ACKNOWLEDGMENTS

I thank my father and stepmother for constantly encouraging and inspiring me to fulfill my dreams. I thank my mother for her continued love and support. I thank my husband for having the insight to recognize the need for this book, and for understanding my love for writing. I thank my daughter for her joyful spirit and her ability to make me smile, especially when the contents of this book began to make me downhearted.

I thank my brother whose appreciation has given me the strength to be the best I can be. I thank my two sisters whose innocent, curious minds gave me the courage to speak the truth. I thank the Gledhills for admiring my words and enthusiastically wanting to read more of them. I thank my grandmothers for believing in me.

Special thanks to my editor, Meredith Puff Hofmann, whose advice guided me throughout the creation of this book and whose talent I greatly respect. Lets do it again soon. I thank my agent, Julie Castiglia whose expertise is a privilege to learn from. I thank my close and supportive friend Jackie Harmon, who diligently and thoroughly gathered much of the important psychological research for this book. I thank Pam Warren for helping me organize the many research references within the book. I thank Fairview Press for specializing in family books and being excited to publish this one.

I thank all of the researchers and writers whose information has contributed tremendously to this book. I thank those who gave their time to be interviewed and allowed their stories to be revealed. I also thank you, the reader, for your interest in this important topic.

TORN TOGAS

ΠΔΣΩΠΔΣΩΠΔΣΩΠΔΣΩΠΔΣΩΠΔΣ

INTRODUCTION

Standing somberly outside a large colonial-styled sorority house with the other rushees, I felt my insides tighten. Had my blood circulation stopped? Slightly nauseous, I tried to breathe slowly, deeply, as we stood under the blazing California sun. It seemed the rush party would never begin.

But it was no wonder my anxiety was so extreme—almost uncontrollable—now, at this crucial moment. I just *had* to find the perfect home away from home, my new "family." I had spent years waiting to find it. Being selected by the right group was critical, so every party I attended was the most important event of my life.

I was terrified of what would happen if I didn't get into a top sorority. I knew I would be an outcast on campus. I'd have no friends for the rest of my college career, and I'd be a disappointment to my parents. I had to make it!

Too nervous to smile, I surveyed my competition. We were all decorated with lots of make-up, hair spray, fancy jewelry, nail polish, hose, and high heels. I hoped my expensive designer dress would score lots of points with the sorority sisters. Over and over in my mind, I planned how to field any questions I might face during the party.

A rude shout interrupted my thoughts. A large group of guys were on the lawn of the fraternity house across the street, drinking beer and gawking at us.

"You in the pink—nice legs!" they whistled. "Come here, baby, give me a kiss. You in the blue! Ten, you're a ten!"

As their heckling continued, I despised them for breaking my concentration at such a crucial time. Just as beads of sweat began forming on my nose and forehead, the doors to the sorority house opened. Beautiful and radiant, the sorority sisters lined up on the porch wearing sky blue, straight, knee-length dresses and singing a slow, sentimental song about their sorority. Deeply moved, I felt tears come to my eyes. I longed to be part of the sisterhood they shared.

As the song ended, they walked down the walkway to greet us, smiling and cheerful. Two perfectly beautiful blonde women put their arms through mine, told me their names and began leading me into their house. They were so gorgeous, I started to worry. Was I pretty enough to get into their sorority?

When my last rush party ended and I was accepted into one of the houses of my choice, I was elated. I belonged! As a new pledge for the next term, I threw myself wholeheartedly into what is known on college campuses as the "Greek system": parties, dates, fund-raisers, sisterhood—all with my new sorority family.

But as time went on, the idyllic sisterhood didn't seem as glamorous as it once appeared. In the midst of all the fun, the Greek system had a dark side.

Frequently I was put into circumstances where I was forced to witness or do things that made me feel uncomfortable. Any doubts or objections I had were either hushed or brushed aside in the name of "Greek tradition."

Pressure to conform was never higher. I felt compelled to dress, speak, and act in a manner that met sorority approval. This approval reigned over my friendships as well. It was frowned upon to talk to someone from a lesser sorority; even worse, to a "non-Greek." And the consequence for not measuring up could be drastic: expulsion from sisterhood.

Greek organizations have a history of excluding not only

those who do not fit their house image, but minorities as well. Yet while peer conformity was and is an accepted part of Greek life, no one likes to think about the incidents that are swept under the rug—namely, gang rapes in fraternity houses, as well as serious injuries or even deaths resulting from drinking games or pledge "hazing."

As it turns out, these incidents are much more common than I had ever dreamed. I would also discover that nearly all Greek houses subject their new pledges to physical abuse and humiliation as a part of hazing, the testing phase and rite of passage necessary to become full-fledged brothers or sisters. Greek life often involves drinking, illegal drug use, and irresponsible and abusive sexual behavior, creating lifelong substance abusers while spreading diseases and increasing the incidents of rape. Discrimination against women, sexual harassment, and sexist attitudes are also common in many houses, especially fraternities. Intense competition between houses, and even between brothers or sisters from the same house, often results in gang fights, eating disorders, the use of steroids, and plastic surgery.

But to overwhelmed, vulnerable pledges who just want a place to make new friends, this dark side is invisible. Having just left home, family, and friends, they look to the Greek system for security and belonging. At worst, they expect fraternities to resemble those of the hit movie *Animal House*. They don't realize that the situation today is far worse than that of the obnoxious drunk pranksters portrayed in the movie. They don't know that along with the benefits of Greek life, they may be forced into situations that threaten their morals. They may face humiliating abuse or even rape, all in the name of "good fun." If nothing else, they will become well schooled in the ways of elitist snobbery.

When new students arrive on campus, the Greek system often appears as the only social network available. Fearing they will miss out on the "total college experience," new students often feel pressured to join. Fraternities and sororities have different systems for rush, but joining always means submitting to a series of parties in which the brightest, best looking, wealthiest, and most polished are sought after for membership. If you don't make it, sorry. Never mind that they never got to know the real you.

Most pledges know little about the sorority or fraternity they pledge other than what they see during the short week of rush parties. Many, like myself, pledge a sorority or fraternity at a vulnerable time in their lives and quickly become entangled by the Greek mindset and the need to conform. Searching for a new identity, and being away from parental values for the first time, students are often wide open to adopting even the lowest of Greek values. Never mind that those values might smack of superficiality, sexual aggression, and abuse. It's all considered the "in" thing to do.

Today, about four hundred thousand men and two hundred fifty thousand women are members of the Greek system. In the U.S. alone, 8.5 million college graduates have been members. How many of them are really satisfied with the experience? After seeing so many unsuspecting students join the Greek system only to find it was not what they expected, I knew this book must be written. Students contemplating Greek life deserve to know what sorority and fraternity life really entails after the happy songs and smiles of rush parties end.

Besides telling my own story, I have conducted countless interviews with actual members who describe their experiences and discuss in depth the internal problems of the Greek system. Extensive research has uncovered case studies and statistics that support these personal accounts.

This book gives students and interested parents the opportunity to understand the hidden side of Greek life, before joining. It thoroughly examines how far the Greek system has departed from the humanitarian and intellectual values upon which they were founded.

For previous members of a Greek organization, this book

provides an opportunity to reevaluate the structural problems of the Greek system and discusses possible ways to bring change; it presents a long-overdue challenge to reform this destructive system which is molding our future leaders. For those still entrapped by the Greek mindset, I hope this book will evoke the conclusion that it's never too late to change destructive Greek traditions, or get out of the system.

1
HAZING
HAZARDOUS TO
YOUR HEALTH

One night I was at a fraternity house visiting my boyfriend while the fraternity's twenty-some pledges scurried about the house, cleaning under the direction of the rest of the brothers. I knew cleaning was only one of the duties required of pledges during their three-month trial period, to prove their worth and loyalty to the group. But I was surprised when one of the brothers began shouting at the top of his voice.

"Line up, maggots!" he yelled at the pledges. "Get in pledge order, now!"

Quick to obey, the pledges gathered from all over the house to line up, from shortest to tallest, with their chins on their chests.

"Watch this!" my boyfriend whispered to me, obviously enjoying the scene as he went to join the gathering group of actives (full-fledged fraternity members). I tried to appear inconspicuous as the actives began circling the line of pledges, randomly yelling obscenities at them.

"You are all such —— losers!" one shouted. "This house still looks like ——! You'll never make it here. I can't believe we have to put up with such idiots!"

One of the brothers handed a bottle of whiskey to the pledge at the front of the line. "Drink up, you wimps!" he ordered. One by one, each took a swig and passed it on until it reached the end. Then the actives took it to the start of the line and the process began all over again.

The smell of alcohol had been thick in the room before the lineup began, and I could tell most of the brothers were already drunk. I observed the glee on their faces as they lorded it over the pledges. But it got even worse.

One of the actives brought out a bucket of smelly, rotten eggs from the kitchen and they all began throwing them at the pledges. To my amazement, the pledges didn't even flinch.

"Pledge Clark, who are our founding fathers?" barked one brother.

A shorter pledge took a step forward and began nervously rambling some names.

"Wrong!" barked the brother again. He then sucked all the mucus out of his throat and spit into the pledge's face. I'd seen enough. Creeping out of the room, I tried not to feel guilty myself. I felt sorry for the pledges.

When I questioned my boyfriend about it later, he laughed it off. "Oh, they're wimps compared to what we went through," he jeered.

At the time, it was hard to understand why the pledges accepted this kind of abuse. What about a fraternity made it worth such humiliation? But as I got more involved in the Greek system, I would learn that these lineups are one of the mildest forms of a wide range of hazing activities most pledges must endure. If they refuse, they won't gain the coveted status of fraternity brother or sorority sister—a goal they will often do anything to achieve.

Hazing is defined by the Fraternity Executives Association as "any action taken or situation created, intentionally, whether on or off fraternity premises, to produce mental or physical discomfort, embarrassment, harassment, or ridicule." A long-standing tradition in the Greek system, hazing is accepted as normal treatment toward pledges who are earning the right to belong.

My first introduction to the hazing lineup was appalling, and as time passed, I saw more and more hazing incidents, first when I was a Little Sister to a fraternity and later when I pledged a sorority myself. Gradually I began to justify such behavior. I came to think that because everyone else approved of hazing as an expected part of pledging, it must be fine.

Not until I graduated and was out on my own did I realize I'd been entangled in a belief system gone awry. Brothers and sisters don't have to dish out verbal, emotional, or physical abuse. They don't have to lord it over one another, or treat one another like slaves. Likewise, those on the receiving end don't have to take that kind of treatment.

What kind of lessons are we learning when surrounded by such an environment? I've observed that rather than change the system once they become members, the once-abused pledges simply take revenge on the next crop of newcomers, devising even more insidious methods of abuse. And so the cycle of abuse continues, getting worse with each pledge class.

Perhaps that's why the incidents of humiliation and abuse often result in hospitalization and even death. Since 1978, the Committee to Halt Useless College Killings (CHUCK) has counted at least sixty-five deaths attributed to fraternity and sorority hazing. Hundreds of other students have been seriously injured, according to Eileen Stevens, founder of the organization, who lost her son, Chuck Stenzel, in a hazing incident in 1978. She claims that most of the deaths and injuries are kept quiet by the organizations or universities to avoid adverse publicity.[1]

In this chapter, we will look at examples of the milder forms of hazing as well as those more extreme. But first, let's examine the Greek system itself.

THE SYSTEM

New pledges in fraternities and sororities quickly learn they are obligated to conform to a certain mold during their three-month trial period. If they don't, they could be dropped at any time, in which case they are referred to as "dung." They learn that their acceptance and self-worth are based not on who they really are, but on their ability to measure up and their capacity to withstand abuse. Greek members believe that pledges should be willing to make any sacrifice requested of them or they are not worthy to become members.

The irony is that during a time when students are exposed to the new and diverse thoughts and lifestyles of college life, they are simultaneously required to fit into a singular, confining mold, denying their own self-expression.

Unfortunately for pledges, that mold often includes elements of slavery during their trial semester. In both fraternities and sororities, pledges are usually considered servants, and can be asked at any time to clean the house, wash cars, do laundry, type papers, or anything else desired by members. Fraternities are typically more extreme than sororities, but both groups make pledging a difficult test of endurance. One fraternity member said he felt like a servant twenty-four hours a day during his pledge period. The fraternity brothers would call him at three in the morning, ordering him to buy some burritos and bring them to the fraternity house. If he didn't comply immediately, his whole pledge class would later be reprimanded in a lineup.

In effect, pledges are the reason fraternities and sororities are able to do what they do best: hold elaborate parties and support philanthropic organizations. Pledges spend days decorating and cleaning before a house party, then at the party aren't allowed to socialize or drink. Instead, they serve drinks, clean up, and take care of their drunk brothers. And pledges are often the ones who fulfill the hours fraternities and sororities are required to volunteer for charitable causes. Yet there is no such thing as sweat equity in the Greek system; pledges are still required to pay full pledge dues. My sorority's fee for the pledge semester was $2,500, with no exceptions (a typical amount).

Nevertheless, pledges are convinced their servitude is a privilege, as is the chance to become full-fledged actives at the end of the semester. What they don't realize—as I didn't, until later—is that they are actually sacrificing all their free time during the pledge semester with no assurance they will be accepted at the end.

Most Greek members believe that pledges need to be humbled before they are allowed to receive the ultimate honor of becoming a member. And actives use this belief to warrant putting pledges in unethical situations.

"There were quite a few lineups when the actives loved urinating all over us," a recent fraternity pledge confided. "They would laugh at us while we were trying to drink our beer, kick sand in our face, and drop buckets of water on us. When we finished our beers, we were forced to repeat the process. You would think they were having the time of their lives."

Sororities also haze pledges, but from my experience and research it's usually more psychologically humiliating than physically harmful. However, several pledges from a sorority recount a hazing incident that involved both physical and emotional abuse.

One night at three in the morning, the pledges were assigned to retrieve framed composite pictures off the walls of a number of fraternities. The catch was, they were only allowed to wear T-shirts and underwear for the errand.

Arriving at the first fraternity house, they found the front door wide open. Assuming everyone was asleep, they crept inside only to be met by a group of at least ten brothers running down the stairs. They'd been set up!

Ignoring the women's struggles and screams, the brothers forcibly shoved them into cold showers and then took them outside to be rolled around in a sandy volleyball court. Only then were they allowed to go back to meet their big sisters at the sorority house.

"When we got back, they lined us up and individually ridiculed us, making references to our weight, bra size, nose size, dress size, and any other physical irregularities," one of the pledges recalled. "I remember being freezing cold and shivering for hours while they made fun of us."

A fraternity brother described similar abuse. While still a pledge, he had returned to his college apartment early during Christmas break. Some of the brothers found out he had returned early, so they invited him and another pledge over for a few beers, with the promise not to treat them as pledges on account of the holidays. But during a drinking game, the scene turned ugly when one of the actives threw a beer bottle against the wall just above the pledge's head. The actives began yelling obscenities at the two pledges, forcing them to stand against the wall and accusing them of not showing enough pledge unity.

"They took us into the garage, made us take off our shirts, and tied our hands up over our heads," the pledge explained. "Then they took turns swinging a paddle and slamming ping-pong balls against our chest at close range. They hit me so hard that the pain made me cry and welts formed on my chest."

Such verbal and physical abuse is commonplace in the Greek system of hazing, transforming otherwise nonviolent students into sadistic bullies who revel in demeaning others. Somehow the group dynamic seems to give permission for otherwise civil and considerate people to behave in a manner they would never even consider under ordinary circumstances.

HELL WEEK

The final week of the fraternity pledge period is traditionally called Hell Week. The week is designed to combine all the hazing activities of the semester into one, very intense week. Oftentimes, tolerance is pushed to the limit in a final test of loyalty where pledges might literally be forced to fight for their lives.

Traditionally, fraternities save the worst hazing for Hell Night, the last night before the initiation ceremony. Hell Night shenanigans come in all forms. At their mildest, pledges are embarrassed and humiliated; at their most extreme, pledges are pushed to such limits that many are hospitalized or even die. Such is the case with many drinking games, which frequently result in alcohol poisoning.

A close friend told me that his clearest memory of hazing wasn't physically harmful; it was something he later learned was called the "dog lick." Pledges were told to remove their clothing and get in a line. All the lights were on, brightly revealing each pledge's naked body as he obeyed the order to get down on all fours, facing the naked behind of the pledge in front of him.

"Suddenly I realized what I was going to have to do," my friend recounted. "Our Hell Master had a leather whip, and whipped us one by one when it was our turn.

"I couldn't see my other pledge brothers performing the 'dog lick,' but as soon as I felt a warm, hard tongue swipe through the crack of my butt, I knew I would really have to do it!

"I don't know how, but I licked my pledge brother's hairy butt. It was so sick! I can't comprehend why I did the things I did just to get into my fraternity."

Another friend in the same fraternity recounted how he and his fellow pledges had to wear white T-shirts, dyed purple underwear, and old, worn overalls for the entire Hell Week and weren't allowed to change their clothes. They were forbidden to brush their teeth, shower, shave, or do any kind of personal grooming. If they wanted to eat, they were given disgusting food, such as a mixture of mint-flavored apple jelly, raw scallops, raw eggs, chard, and Spam. Other entrees included sardines, large chunks of blue cheese washed down with live gold-fish, and chunks of chewing tobacco.

Pledges who protested were told if they didn't eat it, they would wear it—a powerful incentive, since they weren't allowed to shower or change their clothes.

When the pledges were fortunate enough to get a real meal, it usually was a hamburger that had been stepped on, spit on, and soaked in hot sauce. If they didn't eat it within two minutes, the leftovers were tossed into a large bucket of oven-hot malt liquor which was then poured onto the floor. The pledges were commanded to roll around on the floor to "clean up" the malt liquor while eating any remaining pieces of food particles.

Another friend reported that throughout Hell Week he was forced to wear a pompano fish in his underwear. The fish was about four inches long and three inches wide, and the first day it broke open, filling his underwear with guts. Because fraternity brothers periodically asked him to show his pompano, he couldn't remove it. As the week wore on and the smell grew stronger, he said he grew so disgusted it was emotionally exhausting.

The same friend recounted that during lineups, the Hell Master often cracked a raw egg over the head of the first pledge and poured the yolk into the pledge's mouth. The pledge was then commanded to pass the yolk mouth to mouth to the next kneeling pledge, and so on down the line of twenty or so pledges. If the yolk broke, the pledge receiving it had to swallow it, and a new yolk had to be passed from the beginning. Pledges were forced to pass a cube of butter in the same way.

My friend also said the Hell Master, chosen for the week by his fraternity brothers, often blindfolded the pledges, breathed on them, and glided a knife along their necks, saying, "You're dead, pledge!" This particular master, whom my friend describes as huge, enjoyed using his deep, threatening voice to frighten the pledges while he forced them to do repulsive activities.

During the week, the pledges were prevented from getting any more than the minimum amount of sleep needed to survive.

After they fell asleep for a short time, active members would wake them for another lineup.

It was also common, my friend reports, for pledges to be set up to watch a pornographic movie in a dark room—something they might normally have enjoyed—but they were only allowed to watch it in their underwear. At a particularly graphic moment in the movie, the brothers would turn on the lights and begin measuring and ridiculing the size of the pledges' penises. They also kept four sheep around the house, using them to scare pledges into believing they would be forced to have sex with the animals.

SORORITY HELL WEEK

By its very name and purpose, Hell Week would not exist without hazing. In recent years, when sorority headquarters began issuing punishments for chapters participating in hazing, sororities changed the name to Inspiration Week (INSPO). Deemed a week of fun activities to the outside world, INSPO still includes a final night of hazing, however, a night which is hidden from the national organizations.

If pledges make it through an entire pledge semester, they are usually willing to do anything asked of them in the last week. If they comply, the last day is devoted to a long-awaited initiation ceremony that officially makes them members.

These ceremonies contain the unveiling of secret meanings and mysterious symbols that pledges must swear never to reveal. Sororities stress this ritual throughout the pledge semester to keep their pledges in suspense. Through talking to many sorority members, I've learned that these mystical rituals are all based on common humanitarian principles.

While hazing in sororities is usually milder, there are plenty of instances where pledges are required to perform inappropriate, and even dangerous, acts.

One of my own hazing experiences happened in a small bedroom in the sorority house. Surrounded by a group of sorority sisters, the other pledges and I sat in a circle around a stack of *Hustler* magazines, a telephone, and a Greek telephone directory.

"Who'll go first?" one of the members asked. No one responded, so she picked the woman next to me.

"We'll dial a number and I want you to read this in a sexy voice. Your name will be Rhonda." She opened one of the magazines and pointed to a particular paragraph.

The pledge took the magazine while everyone giggled.

"The first call is to Tom Parker," the sister said, dialing the number and handing the phone to the pledge. Tom was considered one of the more popular guys in the Greek system.

"Is Tom Parker there? Oh, hi, Tom, this is Rhonda, the girl you met last weekend." She began speaking slowly, in a deep tone of voice. "I wanted to say that I want you to come over right now. You make me so hot! Just thinking about your big, strong muscles makes me melt. I want to suck on your ——."

The paragraph seemed to go on endlessly. Each new sentence was more obscene than the last.

"I'm on my way over to your place right now!" she finished, and quickly hung up the phone.

"Good job! Now it's your turn, Esther." One of the actives handed me a magazine, pointed to the paragraph, and dialed. I could feel my face turn red and sweaty just thinking about what I would have to do. The fear of being unsuccessful at disguising my voice made me start to shake. When they handed me the phone, my body was numb, but somehow my mouth began reading. It took all my energy to concentrate on reading the again seemingly endless paragraph replete with sleazy, disgusting suggestions. When I could finally hang up, I was relieved.

The sorority sisters thought this was funny. They enjoyed watching us squirm. But to those of us at their mercy it was frightening and demeaning. By this time, however, the other pledges and I had invested so much into joining the sorority that we felt we had no choice but to comply with their demands.

HAZING

During our months of pledging we continually heard how glad we should be that our pledge class had it so much easier than previous classes.

"We had to find our way back to school after being dropped off downtown, drunk," they would say. "Be glad your pledge class never had to do that!"

On the last evening of INSPO, we pledges were blindfolded, put into groups, and led up two flights of stairs into a room. Someone grabbed my shoulders from behind, moved me to a certain place in the room, and instructed me to kneel on the floor.

Suddenly, low, scary whispers came from around the room, sounding something like, "Isnap, isnap, isnap . . . ." What could it mean?

When my blindfold was removed, I saw that four other pledges and I were kneeling in a circle, a foot apart; sorority sisters were standing above us, surrounding us and chanting. The room was lit only by a few candles in the center of our circle, where I immediately noticed a needle, toothpicks, a shot glass, and five pansy crowns with the stems removed.

Amid the continued chants, the sorority president knelt down with us.

"It takes an amazing woman to be worthy of becoming a part of our house," she began. "You must be willing to put your sisters first and sacrifice for us, bonding with us in every way."

She took the needle and pricked her finger. When blood welled out, she quickly placed her finger inside the shot glass, allowing five drops to trickle down the side and settle on the bottom.

"This will create an inseparable bond," she said, stopping the bleeding with a handkerchief. She suddenly turn to a pledge. "What is my name?"

"Ashley."

The president turned to the next pledge and pointed to a member behind her. "What is her name?" There were at least seventy-five members and pledges in the sorority—too many names to learn during a three-month semester.

"Tiffany?" came the tentative answer.

"Wrong!" the president said firmly. "You must begin." She handed her the needle and shot glass. The pledge's eyes quickly widened in fear, but she had no choice. Pricking her finger, she added her five drops of blood to the glass.

The needle, shot glass, and handkerchief were passed to all five of us pledges while the rest of the sorority chanted, "isnap, isnap, isnap . . . ." Our blood collected, the president put the blood-stained shot glass in the center of our circle. She turned to me.

"What does 'isnap' mean?"

"I don't know," I admitted. The president turned to the other pledges.

"Can any of you tell me the meaning?"

A friend sitting next to me nervously whispered the answer, but no one heard her.

"This is disappointing." She picked up a pansy crown. "Each of you take a pansy, put some blood on it, and put it on your finger."

To demonstrate, she dipped a toothpick into the bloody glass, rubbed it onto the pansy, and then wiped the blood-stained pansy onto her pricked finger. The shot glass slowly made its way around the circle of sorority members above us.

"Now you will make an effort to join our bond of sister-hood," the president announced. "I remind you that the pansy is our sacred flower and represents the joining of selected sisters. 'Isnap' is 'pansy' backwards."

They all took turns mixing each other's blood and rubbing it back on their fingers, using the pansy. Fear began to overcome me. I just couldn't stick my finger with a needle and mix my blood with that of these women I barely knew. What if I faint? What if I contract AIDS?

"You can go first," she ordered one of my pledge sisters who looked scared. I started feeling sick to my stomach as I watched the president take the glass from one of the other members and hand it to my pledge sister, who slowly placed the glass on the floor.

Just as she lifted the needle to prick her finger, the door opened and another sorority member told us, "come on, your group needs to hurry to get to the next event."

The sorority members seemed disappointed as we got up and began to get blindfolded. We were off to experience more hazing during an evening my pledge sisters and I thought we should be getting rewarded for meeting the requirements to become new members.

THE RATIONALE

Why do pledges put up with hazing? It would seem that the fear of not belonging causes them to participate. Most pledges place as high an importance on getting into a house as on getting into college. Oftentimes it is more than their own desire to get in; they receive pressure from family members or friends to join a particular fraternity or sorority. Parents or even siblings might have been members of the Greek system and might have high hopes that their kids will continue the tradition. Or, friends might convince students that a social life will be virtually nonexistent unless they get into a particular house, or, if they already belong to a house, friends might threaten to end relationships with non-Greeks.

In his book *Victims of Groupthink*, Yale psychology professor emeritus Irving L. Janis states that there is an enormous fear of refusing to comply, because "to refuse puts one in danger of being a deviant by violating a group norm."[2] Though they may not agree with the group's behavior, members go along with it to avoid rejection.

In a study of hazing published in the *Journal of Abnormal and Social Psychology*, authors Elliott Aronson and Judson

Mills report that a pledge who survives a severe ordeal will probably find membership in a group all the more appealing. If they do what they must to get in, the group to which they aspire has value. Therefore, what is asked of them cannot be so unreasonable. Besides, they ask, didn't the other members go through it?

Initiates have an overwhelming need to understand how they fit into the world, Aronson and Mills write. If this need is not addressed regularly, frustration and stress from dissonance occur. Once the initiates envision themselves as part of the Greek world, they feel dissonance if they believe something might deprive them of being part of the group.[3]

There is also a feeling of privilege that goes along with hazing. Pledges rationalize that if they have to suffer and face difficult challenges to get into the group, they must be privileged, simply because they are capable of enduring such suffering. Perhaps that is why many Greeks brag about hazing rituals they've endured, as if they were telling a type of war story.

In his dissertation on fraternity Hell Week, sociologist Milton Glenn Walker compares the group solidarity that arises from fraternity hazing with that of military boot camp. He cites an anonymous article from the *American Journal of Sociology,* "The Making of an Infantry Man," that says: "It is out of the agonies of training that [infantry soldiers] develop pride in having done what they believe many of their former friends could not have done and which they themselves never thought they could do."[4]

In a recent study of sorority rush, researchers found there are vast differences between independent and Greek students. Members of the Greek system had significantly less "independence, liberalism, social conscientiousness, and cultural sophistication" than the independent students, and tended to be "higher in sociability, hedonism, self-confidence, and social conformity." The study also found that Greek organizations actively recruit pledges who are similar to themselves.[5] Perhaps this is yet another reason pledges comply with unreasonable hazing requirements.

THE CYCLE OF REVENGE

To become a full-fledged brother or sister, pledges undergo an enormous ordeal. The sense of accomplishment and belonging that accompanies membership is enormous—as is their need for revenge. What is so ironic, though, is on whom this revenge is sought. Seemingly, there is a shift from perpetrator to victim, from the "in" crowd to the "out." Rather than retaliate against those who made them suffer, newly initiated brothers and sisters seek new victims for their revenge: the next pledge class. And the next phase of hazing frequently yields far worse abuse. I have seen many pledges vow to end hazing once they become actives, only to become some of the worst hazers themselves. They rationalize that if *they* had to go through it, so does the next pledge class.

Occasionally, however, new members do seek revenge on their perpetrators. Though such acts are rare, one fraternity brother reported that once he and his fellow pledges were initiated, they took revenge by kidnapping three actives from a bar. After tying their brothers up and blindfolding them, the pledge class threw them into cars and drove them to a vacant, dingy apartment building in an impoverished neighborhood.

Fueled by plenty of beer, the pledge class stripped the actives down to their underwear, poured motor oil all over them, forced them to drink excessive amounts of beer, and blew cigar smoke into their faces for four hours, all the while swearing at them. Then, illustrating what they endured during their own pledge period, the pledges asked their captives questions about the fraternity's history, questions so difficult they were nearly impossible to answer. Only when the night was over were the actives allowed to dress and return to the fraternity house.

INJURIES AND DEATHS
ATTRIBUTED TO HAZING

Hazing rituals date back to ancient Greece, with the first hazing-related death reported in 1838 at Franklin Seminary in Kentucky.[6] Besides emotional and psychological hazing, pledges have been made to do so many calisthenics that they were hospitalized; they have had bones broken; and one pledge was even maimed when someone set fire to his beard.[7]

At Syracuse University, a pledge was hospitalized after an active member wearing spiked golf shoes walked on his bare feet.[8] At another New York university, a pledge was paralyzed after diving down a flight of stairs, a widespread hazing practice. Another pledge in Illinois was injured when the wooden coffin he was made to lie in was set on fire.[9] Members of a Minnesota fraternity even used chemicals to burn their insignia on the pledges' backs.[10]

But even with these and other serious hazing injuries, nothing is so tragic as the stories of actual deaths.

The body of Gabriel Benjamin "Gabe" Higgins, a nineteen-year-old University of Texas student, was recovered from the Colorado river on May 4, 1995. An autopsy showed that Higgins's blood-alcohol level was .21, twice the legal driving limit of .10, and that he had drowned. The Bastrop County Sheriff's Department received several anonymous calls saying that Higgins was a victim of hazing.

Higgins, who was a pledge for a University of Texas spirit club called the Texas Cowboys, was swimming with club members at a Cowboy event called a "picnic." "Picnics historically include drinking games and the paddling of pledges, the *Austin American-Statesman* reported. The Cowboys are on probation through August for a 1994 hazing incident that involved paddling at an initiation ceremony." Paddling and forced drinking, suspected activities of the picnic, are considered illegal hazing under state law.[11]

Another tragedy is the story of Michael Davis. When Davis

called his girlfriend on February 14, 1994, he had more to say than "Happy Valentine's Day." The twenty-five-year-old Kappa Alpha Psi fraternity pledge said he was in pain from a beating he'd received from five brothers punching and kicking him. When his girlfriend asked if he ever got the urge to swing back, he simply answered, "We can't."

The next day, the brothers were going down the lineup, again punching and hitting the pledges, when Michael collapsed. Not realizing the severity of his injuries, the brothers didn't take him to the hospital until it was too late. He was pronounced dead from a blow to the head.[12]

THE BATTLE AGAINST HAZING

Michael Davis is only one of the latest in a long line of hazing deaths. Similar incidents in the past have resulted in a mere slapping on the wrist of participants, but largely because of new antihazing campaigns, one of the most extensive criminal hazing prosecutions in history followed Michael's death. As a result, a total of sixteen people were charged under Missouri's state antihazing law, and seven were charged with involuntary manslaughter. As of the writing of this book, the case is still in the courts.[13]

Eileen Stevens founded the Committee to Halt Useless College Killings (CHUCK) after the 1978 death of her son, Chuck Stenzel. His story is recorded in Hank Nuwer's book *Broken Pledges*. While a pledge of Klan Alpine fraternity at Alfred University in upstate New York, Chuck was locked in the trunk of a car and told to drink a pint of whiskey while the brothers drove around on a freezing night. Afterward, Chuck participated in typical fraternity drinking games where pledges were told to fill a garbage can with their vomit.[14]

Chuck died hours later of alcohol poisoning. His blood alcohol level was .46, more than four times the legal limit.

Since then, Eileen Stevens has become a national spokeswoman against hazing, lobbying state legislatures for antihazing laws and working with the families of those killed in hazing-related incidents.

When Chuck Stenzel died in 1978, only three states had antihazing laws. Today, antihazing laws have been passed in at least thirty-nine states, though few are strict enough to carry serious criminal liability or provide sentences strong enough to deter hazing effectively.[15]

Despite recent efforts against hazing, the tradition remains intact. It is so strong, in fact, that many members refuse to stop hazing, and hide the evidence from their universities and national organizations. The organizations that oversee Greek fraternities and sororities on college campuses across the country—the Interfraternity Council or the College Panhellenic Council, respectively—have tried punishing those individuals involved in hazing incidents, but the results have been temporary. Oftentimes, the consequences are minimal. A house might be put on probation, banned from participating in rush, or forbidden to have parties for a semester.

For reports of severe hazing, punishment can take the form of suspension, but that, too, stops hazing for only a short time. Members return from their suspension being especially careful not to haze pledges, but usually after a few semesters the cycle begins again, and hazing is once again adopted. Eventually, it becomes violent enough that the house is again reported and punished. It is a perpetual cycle. Fraternities and sororities have an understanding: hazing is acceptable—and often encouraged—as long as they don't get caught.

In actuality, fraternities and sororities get away with hazing relatively easily, because they have little supervision. Large groups of often immature students are left practically alone to manage themselves for the first time in their lives, and they can get out of hand. One fraternity member told me that their national headquarters sent someone out to check on them once a semester, but they all knew when the inspector was coming.

During the four or five days he was there, they wined and dined him and kept on their best behavior. "Once he was gone, that was it; we could do anything we wanted," he explained. Sororities are a little more controlled because they usually have live-in house mothers to take care of meals and house maintenance. However, members still have private meetings—without house mothers—where they can perform hazing rituals.

Furthermore, the vast majority of hazing incidents are never reported, especially if victims recover with no permanent bodily injury. Pledges typically do not tell anyone the specifics of hazing rituals, for fear of jeopardizing their new membership. And no college regulations or laws require students to report hazing.

Dr. Mark Taff, the coeditor of a 1985 study of hazing deaths and injuries for the *American Journal of Forensic Medicine and Pathology,* says that the amount of hazing reported is only the tip of the iceberg. All too often, school administrators continue to deny that hazing activities are damaging. And in those rare instances when a fraternity or sorority is punished, it is simply closed down for a semester or two.[16]

Ironically, it is the past victims of hazing, alumni of the Greek system, who can best make the public aware of the hazards of hazing. But as they move into their postcollege lives, most alumni distance themselves from their days in the Greek system. Interestingly enough, according to a survey of alumni and active members, most Greek alumni see no need to change hazing rituals. Researchers found that 77 percent of current members and 63 percent of alumni consider hazing to play an important role in Greek life. Only 10 percent of current members and a mere 13 percent of alumni surveyed considered hazing a problem in their own houses. More than half agreed that hazing "builds pledge class unity."[17]

While the humiliation of hazing is said to build bonds and forge a collective identity, however, it appears that hazing is at least as dividing as it is uniting. "[Fraternities and sororities] try to build a brotherhood and a sisterhood. Beating the tar out of each other is not the best way to do that," said Tim Burke, a Cincinnati attorney whose firm represents several national fraternities and sororities.[18]

THE WAY OF CHANGE

If you find yourself in a hazing situation with which you are uncomfortable, quite simply, do not participate. No affiliation is worth risking loss of life, permanent disfigurement, or psychological and emotional wounding. Legitimate fraternities and sororities do not require a student to do anything that is silly or dangerous in order to become a member. If members are telling you otherwise, talk to the director of Greek affairs at your college and tell him or her what you are being asked to do, before you comply. While reporting hazing incidents will likely be difficult, it is a crucial step in protecting others and creating a safe Greek environment.

Hazing is against the law, so it is strongly addressed by the National Panhellenic Conference and the National Interfraternity Conference. Following suit, chapter houses increasingly encourage members to report any and all hazing incidents. While not always successful, such efforts are helping to reduce the frequency of severe hazing. According to an advisor for the National Panhellenic Conference, when one of its affiliated sororities finds out about hazing the arrant perpetrators are dismissed or put on probation, and the victims supported. If the hazing is a widespread occurrence, the entire chapter is placed on probation. (Reportedly, most hazing is not chapterwide; it is usually a small group of members trying to show off. Therefore, the process of identifying those members involved in hazing is usually a simple one.)

At my own college, when a pledge reported severe hazing, the fraternity was forced not only to accept the entire pledge class as members, but to grant them high-ranking positions within the fraternity as well. The pledge who reported the hazing became the president and was in charge of implementing a new, reliable program for his fraternity. With the support of the chapter, he was able to accomplish a positive change in the system.

Greek organizations and their chapters typically address hazing and other unacceptable rituals though policies and educational programming—namely, magazines, video tapes, and personal visits. University administrators of Greek affairs are encouraged to inform students that hazing is not allowed and urge them to report it, if it should occur. During rush, students are usually informed of their rights, one of which is that they should not tolerate hazing. Chapters are also encouraged to offer programs year-round that specifically address hazing. In general, according to one advisor, these programs try to separate the word *tradition* from the concept of hazing, in an attempt to reduce the practice's long-standing rationale.

Because there is an influx of new students each year, however, the problem of hazing will likely persist. According to a member of the National Panhellenic Conference, several sororities offer thorough, effective hazing prevention programs one year, but do not provide anything the next. "They will sort of slack off," she said, "when, in effect, a [new] college generation needs to hear it all the time."

"My colleagues and I feel that hazing is back with a vengeance," said an advisor for the National Interfraternity Conference. "You think you are making progress, then all of a sudden things just start popping up."

Many suggestions have been made regarding ways to eliminate or lessen incidents of hazing. The National Interfraternity Conference now supports chapters who have abolished or shortened their pledge periods. Those fraternities without a pledge period invite students to become members, and if that person decides to join, he is not required to go through an orientation procedure, but immediately enjoys full rights. "Those fraternities which have moved to a 'no pledging policy' are pretty satis-

fied with the results," reports an advisor to National Interfraternity Conference. "It has, for the most part, eliminated hazing."

Most fraternities still consider a pledge period necessary,
however, because it introduces pledges to the organization and
helps fraternity members get to know their new brothers before
they become members. As a compromise, many fraternities have
reduced the length of time students pledge. Ten years ago, a
pledge period may have lasted eight to ten weeks; today, it typically lasts four to six weeks.

The National Interfraternity Conference also promotes
"membership education," which begins at pledge time and continues throughout members' college careers and even after graduation. All members are involved with such membership education. New members are not asked to do no more than existing
members and there is no subservient level of membership.

Another solution to hazing is being tried by fraternities at
Washington and Lee University in Lexington, Virginia. Using
sorority houses as a model—sorority houses are required to have
a "house mother," a woman who lives in the house and moni-
tors members' activities—these fraternities established live-in
house directors for fraternity houses.

In 1986, after the Phi Gamma house was rebuilt from a fire,
the university began requiring that its fifteen fraternities have
house mothers. The university had this requirement in the
1920s, but the students began complaining that with house
mothers living in the fraternity houses, they were not getting
enough freedom, authority, or independence. In 1971, it was no
longer a requirement. The director of the Greek Affairs Office
told me that since the reimplementation of this system, incidents
of vandalism and hazing have declined, and the members have
taken better care and maintenance of the houses. Other campuses that require fraternities to have house mothers are Ohio State
University, Ohio University, and the University of Arkansas.

Some other ideas that might be considered: require Greek

administrators to make surprise—that is, genuine surprise—visits, and forbid fraternities and sororities across the board to hold any gatherings the week before finals, the period traditionally reserved for Hell Week.

2
SEXISM AND SEXUAL HARASSMENT

Breathing hard and smoothing my hair into place, I tried to act like nothing was wrong as I rejoined my circle of friends at the fraternity party. Music was blaring loudly, and in the spirit of a Hawaiian luau, the women all wore bikini tops and sarongs while the fraternity brothers wore shorts. I tried to laugh and act natural, but my mood no longer matched the festive theme. All I could think about was what had just happened.

It was my sophomore year, and I had been part of the fraternity's Little Sister program for more than a year. So when one of the guys said he had something important to tell me, I believed him, innocently. I thought he was a friend, and he offered consolation and information about the boyfriend who had just broken up with me.

I was completely unprepared for what happened next. Once we were alone outside the fraternity house, my so-called friend pushed me to the ground behind some bushes, forcefully kissing me and trying to pull off my clothes. I struggled to resist and somehow managed to escape his grasp, running back to the party and safety—but not without some scratches and bruises to show for it.

Still badly shaken, I laughed nervously as the group congratulated a friend of mine, who had just won third place in the bathing suit contest. I would never want to be put on display in such a contest, but I played along with the comments and wisecracks. Dusk was starting to fall, and I was glad the darkness now covered my scratches.

"So, Esther," one of the fraternity brothers jeered, "are you going to get thrown into the swamp again this year?"

"Not if I can help it," I answered, rolling my eyes. Every year at the end of the party, the guys threw as many women as they could into their pledge-made swamp. Last year we women had lost most of our clothes in the cold water, then faced the humiliation of trying to find them while fraternity members rated our exposed figures. I was already planning to leave the party early.

Suddenly, a large section of the party began laughing, and we all turned to see why. A sloppy, drunk fraternity member was standing with his jeans on the floor, exposing himself to the crowd.

"Hey, you slutty whores," he taunted with a silly grin. "I know why you are all here. You want a piece of this!" He pointed to his penis and jerked his hips back and forth.

The group of women nearest to him all smiled with embarrassment. He pulled his pants back on and began chanting as he pointed to different women.

"Eenie, meanie, minie, moe, who's going to be the lucky ho'?" With that he grabbed the last woman he pointed to and started kissing her. Laughing, she pushed him away.

Soon the others lost interest and continued on as if nothing had happened. Instead of apologizing for their brother's behavior, the guys we were with told us the crude nickname their brother's large penis had earned him. They explained that he often got his thrills proving how well the name suited him.

No one else seemed troubled; if anything, the others appeared to think it was funny, so I tried to ignore my own feelings of offense. All the same, I was relieved to leave the party early that night, escaping the sexually charged atmosphere and avoiding the dreaded swamp.

I wish I could say it was the last such party I attended, but it wasn't. The more I was around these guys, the more I got used to their sexual wisecracks and behavior. I grew to believe that because this type of behavior was so common and accepted, it must be all right, even normal.

Not until my senior year, while taking a women's studies course, did I begin to realize how the atmosphere around the fraternity was affecting me. Being around constant sexual badgering and prejudiced attitudes toward women had seriously repressed my self-confidence, giving me an unhealthy view of my role as a woman. I had begun to think of myself in the way women were viewed by the fraternity men—as little more than a sex object.

One day, I started telling a fraternity friend about the enlightening material I had been learning in my class, when all at once I began to cry, frustrated and confused. He, being deeply involved with and committed to his fraternity, accused me of overreacting. More clearly than ever, I began to see that the environment I had subjected myself to was extremely unhealthy, not only for women, but also for the men entangled in its mindset. Because sexual aggression so permeates the lifestyle, language, and morals of fraternity members, fraternity houses have become a virtual breeding ground for men indoctrinated into the ways of sexism and sexual harassment.

"I think it continues to be a problem," said a member of the National Interfraternity Conference, "ranging from just individuals having inappropriate attitudes and doing inappropriate things, unfortunately, all the way to institutionalized activities such as a party theme or a T-shirt design."

In her book, *I Never Called It Rape,* Robin Warshaw states

that fraternities teach their members "a group ethos which objectifies and debases women through language and physical aggression, which lauds heavy drinking and other drug use, and which reinforces group loyalty through united behavior."[1] In a group that encourages its members toward an ethos of sexist behavior, it's no wonder few fraternity members show respect for women.

Now let's take a closer look at how sexism and sexual harassment permeate the fraternity lifestyle.

A BREEDING GROUND

"We only wanted girls around for one thing: to be conquered," confided a recent college graduate and fraternity member. The fraternity always made it clear, he said, that they just wanted women around for sex. Only women who understood their purpose were wanted, so they would comply. What's more, if anyone took offense at this view, the fraternity brothers told that person to leave, claiming they were the first to admit they were pigs and they were proud of it.

Other fraternity members confessed that they often made a game out of competing with each other over who could have sex with a certain woman. Most fraternities hold ceremonies where they present awards to those who sleep with the most women in one night, as well as those who have the highest total for the semester. One brother explained it this way: "The biggest studs were the guys who would bone several chicks in one night and let the other guys watch while he did it." Fraternity brothers frequently film women in sex acts without their knowledge; one later sent the videotape to a woman's mother.[2]

Awards are also given to the fraternity member who perform the most disgusting sex act. The fraternity house where I was a Little Sister gave out such an award to a member who had sex with two women passed out in the same soiled bed—one of them had urinated and eliminated feces all over it. This earned one of the women an obscene nickname among the fraternity members, and before long she quit coming to the house.

Such competitive sex awards encourage members toward sexual aggression, applauding the use of women for sex in a most unhealthy atmosphere. One can only wonder what type of man such an environment fosters.

Based on years of associating myself with fraternities, I can recount firsthand the sexist atmosphere present in most fraternity houses. Walking through a typical house, one would find naked women on posters and calendars, or maybe even catch a pornographic movie on the television set. Perhaps most offensive is the crude, degrading language that is so pervasive in fraternities. Simply because we were there, my friends and I were often called every possible vulgar name referring to female body parts or promiscuous women.

Some examples of their language are recorded in *Fraternity Gang Rape: Sex, Brotherhood, and Privilege on Campus,* by Peggy Reeves Sanday, an anthropology professor at the University of Pennsylvania. Fraternity members confided to her that they label women they slept with as "gash, horsebags, heifers, scum, scum bags, queens, swanks, scum buckets, scum doggies, wenches, life-support systems, beasts, bitches, swatches, and cracks."[3] From these examples, it is obvious: speaking to and about women in a dehumanizing way is normal, everyday language at a fraternity.

Another way fraternity members degrade women is by acting as if they have the right to touch areas of a woman's body whenever they choose. In my own experience, it is common for fraternity members to grab or pinch women's buttocks and breasts or to kiss them—without warning or their consent—especially at a party. In their book on peer harassment, J. Hughes and B. Sandler recount the "flying blue max," in which fraternity members position a woman so that one of them can bite her on the bottom. They also describe "sharking," the practice in which a fraternity pledge goes up to an unknown woman and bites her on the breast.[4]

Although these practices are obviously offensive, the majority of fraternity members consider them not only acceptable, but humorous. One fraternity member rationalized, "a girl should know she has a good chance of being felt up now and then—if she's hanging around our house, she probably wants it." Many fraternity members consider the women who hang out with them personal property—especially Little Sisters, as will be discussed later.

STRIPPERS

Several years ago, I attended my sorority's annual weekend event in Palm Springs, California. I was sunbathing by the hotel pool, with hundreds of other Greek members, when all of a sudden, the disc jockey stopped the music to make an announcement over the loud speaker.

No sooner were the words spoken—"The stripper is here!"—than crowds of men dashed inside to get the best seats. For hours, we women were left alone as the guys were otherwise occupied. Did it bother us? Sort of, but the event was so typical we had come to expect it.

By now, we were all well accustomed to fraternities hiring strippers or hookers. Birthdays, pinnings, graduation, a new pledge class, winning an interfraternal football game—just about any event, no matter how insignificant, was reason enough.

Only recently, however, did I learn what went on at the show. Some former fraternity members confessed in an interview that these events were never simply strip shows, but actually involved active sexual participation by each fraternity brother in attendance. Going around the room, each guy was expected to perform different types of sexual acts with the woman while everyone watched. They admitted that if someone didn't want to take a turn, they would usually do it anyway for fear of ridicule or being labeled homosexual.

"It was always much better just to get drunk and hope you wouldn't contract AIDS," one member recounted.

The same pressure to conform is found throughout the entire fraternal system. Many fraternity members have confided that if a brother doesn't comply with the sexist attitudes of the group, he is treated with disrespect. For example, at one fraternity, members ridiculed two guys who were loyal to their girlfriends, and polite and respectful toward women in general. These guys would be labeled "nice guys" by most women, but the fraternity members claimed these guys were just going to get "burned" because "chicks don't like nice guys."

Likewise, monogamy is considered taboo in most fraternities and is a sure way to face derision. "Any girl with a boyfriend in our fraternity would be an idiot if she thought he was loyal to her," claimed one member. He went on to say they were too young to sleep only with their girlfriends, and "besides, girls want a challenge."

He and his friends genuinely believed that if a woman found out her boyfriend was cheating on her, it was her fault for trusting him. Clearly, fraternity brothers who treat women with any respect lose the respect of the others.

THE DOMINANT MALE

Closely linked with such disdain for women is the way in which the Greek system fosters stereotypical views of male dominance and female submissiveness—views that existed over one hundred years ago when fraternities and sororities were founded. A 1991 study verified that members of the Greek system are especially likely to adopt these views, particularly the belief that aggression and dominance are expected in masculine behavior.[5]

If we examine today's Greek system closely, it's apparent that male dominance in fraternities has grown even more pronounced since the system's inception. As a recent study explains, women who participate in fraternal organizations and events today are being used "as bait for new members, as servers of brothers' needs, and as sexual prey."[6]

This is especially true in fraternities' Little Sister or Little Sweetheart programs, the most pronounced sexist structure in the Greek system. At first glance, these auxiliary programs appear to be a nice idea: college and noncollege women are initiated as "mascots" to the fraternity. But upon close examination, the true purpose of these groups becomes obvious: to ensure that fraternity members have an elite collection of beautiful women from which to choose at their parties. In short, these women are objects who exist solely to bring pleasure to the brothers.

To select Little Sisters, fraternities have highly competitive rush parties, invitation lists, and bidding, although there is no limit to the number they may choose. Once they have made their selections, fraternity members continually remind the women of the competition, to make them feel privileged. Like male fraternity members, Little Sisters have a trial pledge period that lasts about a semester, as well as a formal initiation—yet they are considered inferior to male pledges, because they will never be allowed to become actual fraternity members.

Fraternity brothers generally have little or no respect for their Little Sisters, considering them solely responsible for pleasing and supporting the fraternity men. Little Sisters are often used for menial tasks, such as running errands, mending, laundry, baking, holding fund-raisers, and cleaning the fraternity houses for rush. With such obvious male dominance and female subservience, it becomes apparent that Little Sisters exist merely to boost the egos of insecure fraternity men.[7]

Likewise, the role of Little Sisters is also to provide sexist amusement for fraternity members. In some fraternities, Little Sisters take part in an annual "Slave Auction" in which brothers bid on the women for their services (such as cleaning, baking, and chauffeuring). During this auction, in which the highest bidder purchases his "slave for a week," fraternity members encourage the Little Sisters "to get intoxicated and dance seductively on stage in front of them," according to a *Gender & Society* article entitled "'Buddies' or 'Slutties': The Collective Sexual Reputation of Fraternity Little Sisters," which went on to report that fraternity brothers "bid more money and cheered louder for women who simulated sex on a pole erected in the middle of the stage."[8]

Women also play a major part in fraternity rushes, where fraternities compete for new members by making grand promises to provide "all the beautiful women and beer any man could want." The houses may also show rush slide shows featuring Little Sisters in bathing suits, and display posters or brochures with shapely women as the main feature. A chart compiled by one fraternity depicted the number of beers needed to seduce each of their Little Sisters.[9] Another fraternity presented potential members with a full-color glossy booklet containing a centerfold layout of their Little Sisters wearing bathing suits.[10] Fraternities also throw elaborate rush parties with themes such as "Pimp and Hooker" and "Minerva's Period" ("Minerva" being the name given to Little Sisters in one fraternity).[11]

As a Little Sister myself for two years, I can attest that we were not allowed to go to events sponsored by other fraternities unless we had a good excuse. The reason? The houses were so competitive, we were told it made them look bad if we were seen at another fraternity's event. One Little Sister reported being kicked out just for going to another fraternity's rush party.

"They told me that I betrayed them," she said, "and they didn't want to see me around the fraternity house again." They told her if she wanted to go to that fraternity's parties she should join that group instead.

Such a tactic is clearly an attempt to control, one of the strongest elements of male dominance. But the most severe domination of Little Sisters is seen during rites of initiation. These rituals range from mild to severe, and almost always involve heavy drinking. Little Sister pledges are usually willing to comply with anything that is asked of them during their initiation, sometimes doing things most people would consider out of the question.

My own Little Sister initiation was mild in comparison with most, but I had heard so many stories of what could happen that I was fearful for the worst. First we were required to go on an embarrassing scavenger hunt, going to homes of various fraternity members to retrieve a long list of articles such as underwear, condoms, pornography magazines, and similar items. Later that evening, the other pledges and I waited together as we were individually blindfolded and led to a candlelit room. In front of all the fraternity members, I was told to "kneel and drink to Minerva," and was expected to guzzle a pint-sized mug of beer as fast as I could. Although I felt like vomiting afterward, I was relieved that I had gotten off so easy.

One of the most blatantly sexist initiation ceremonies reported involved the entire pledge class being told to wear nothing but their panties and a thin, white T-shirt given to them by fraternity members. While the women waited together in a room by themselves, two at a time were selected to come before the entire fraternity. Telling the women to stand on a picnic table, the men began to sing a fraternity song while both women chugged a pitcher of beer as fast as they could. Then the fraternity president watered the women down with a garden hose, causing their T-shirts to become completely wet and see-through.

Next, each woman was given a banana and told to kneel. As the fraternity sang another song, the women were told to suck on the banana, placing one hand on their breast. Finally, the women were ordered to kiss each other sensuously on the lips, using their tongues. If the kiss wasn't sensual enough, they had to do it until the fraternity members finally clapped with approval and awarded them their Little Sister pins.

With reports such as these, the Little Sisters arrangement is finally coming under criticism by the National Panhellenic

Conference and other college students. Through many testimonies of graphic and outlandish behavior, it's finally becoming acknowledged that Little Sisters programs bring the opportunity for sexual harassment, discrimination, and even rape, as will be discussed in the next chapter. The name itself, "Little Sisters," firmly reinforces the view that the women are there to be exploited, placing them in subordinate positions. Although created to be a social outlet for women, these auxiliary groups have become demeaning and outdated as the emphasis on women's rights and opportunities widen.

THE STAGE

Most college advisors would agree that forbidding women to go where they choose, touching them in private areas, or calling them crude, belittling names while using offensive language would constitute sexual harassment. However, it appears that most college advisors have never recognized the harm in annual or biannual fraternity events that set the stage for such behavior. While these events are supposedly designed as social celebrations to proclaim fraternity pride and brotherhood, they also provide an arena for women to be put in humiliating and subservient positions.

I remember watching many events that were blatantly sexist, amazed that the school and the sorority members approved of them. These week-long parties customarily had loud music and free-flowing beer, and the usual relay races and events always seemed to focus on watching women make fools of themselves by submitting to ridiculous tasks created by fraternity members. For example, the finale of one relay race involved splashing through a huge mud puddle, invariably causing the women to look like mud wrestlers in skimpy outfits. Likewise, the date auction put women in the questionable position of spending an evening with a man they likely did not know, or trust.

One of the most famous of such national events is the Sigma

Chi Derby Days, a competition among the university's sororities sponsored by the Sigma Chi fraternity. According to the 1990 *U.S.C. Derby Days Magazine,* the same competitions are held at this event across the country.

First, the "Derby Doll Pageant" consists of women modeling bikinis and evening gowns. Next, the "Is She Dizzy?" event is a five-woman relay race requiring each woman to run the length of the beach, pick up a bat and spin around ten times. Another event, the "Betty Bash," requires two sorority members to balance on a beam above the water and pummel each other with spongy Nerf clubs until one falls in.[12]

These and the thirteen other events may appear to be "all in good fun," but in actuality they degrade, belittle, and dehumanize women. *U.S.C. Derby Days Magazine* also describes how points are awarded to women who go to the local tanning booth or show up at a certain bar to drink, and for "dubious deeds, such as practical jokes and general styling" (brown-nosing). Basically, these award-winning deeds can comprise anything done for the fraternity captains, as long as it is not illegal, and could include sexual favors.[13]

ENTRAPMENT

As we have seen, the very structure of fraternities provides a breeding ground for sexism and sexual harassment, facilitating unacceptable behavior and attitudes. Some argue that fraternities and sororities are constitutionally sexist because they restrict admission by gender.[14] The fact that Greek members are more accepting of gender-role stereotyping and discrimination is widely acknowledged and well documented. What is less tangible is the belief that this sexist mindset stems from insecurity. Nevertheless, it is a belief highly probable, and one that is attracting attention.

In *Fraternity Gang Rape: Sex, Brotherhood, and Privilege on Campus,* Peggy Reeves Sanday reports a study that found that men who are more insecure than average are attracted to fraternities. These men often have not yet broken their psychological and social bonds to their parents, especially to their mothers, and are unconsciously drawn to the security promised by the fraternity "alter ego." Acceptance into a fraternity gives these young men the secured self-confidence they desire, providing they fit the so-called "masculine" mold and adopt the sexist attitudes of their fellow fraternity brothers. In an intensely competitive culture, the act of degrading women unites them; it gives them a group identity. And, as we saw in the last chapter, pledges comply with tightly enforced rules of conformity while enduring humiliating and painful hazing and initiation rites, simply to find that promise of self-assurance—the coveted niche on campus.[15] In an article for *Ms.* magazine, Andrew Merton explains that for many young men, college is their first experience with independence and developing their "manhood." This transition—which often manifests itself in self-acceptance at the expense of others dissimilar—causes them to view women only as objects for sexual defeat who are suitable, but inferior rivals. "The idea of women as equals is strange and inconvenient at best, terrifying at worst," Merton writes. Clearly, fraternities provide a haven perfectly suited to intensify these prejudices.[16]

However, just as it is hard for us to accept that educated men encourage such sexism in the Greek system, it is equally hard to understand why women accept, and often condone, not only gender-role stereotyping, but also such explicitly sexist, objectification. Here, too, insecurity could be the culprit. Because these women are more insecure than average, they are more eager to conform to sorority norms, and with such conformity goes a substantial reduction in the "likelihood that one will express or even contemplate discomfort or concern."[17] For most, it is easier to conform than to express feelings.

In a new environment, young women like me try to feel self-confident and accepted by others, especially by men. Without a strong and healthy understanding of their own self-worth prior to college, women may easily become confused. By seeing across-the-board acceptance of male dominance and female sub-missiveness within the Greek system, women are influenced to believe that these are the roles of society.

Many young women are still socialized to find their security through men's opinions of them. A study in 1984 showed that many women today believe they are "passive sexual receptors," as opposed to men, who view themselves as "active sexual agents."[18] If a woman's self-worth is based upon her desirability as a sex object, it is not surprising that so many women willingly accept gender-role stereotyping and prejudices against them.

POSITIVE STEPS

Houses would likely benefit by requiring their members to take a seminar on sexism and sexual harassment. The National Fraternity Conference provides such material to fraternities across the country, in which students work through case studies containing sexist situations that they may not have confronted before. By using these case studies and similar education, frater-nity members learn what kinds of things are considered sexist, and are therefore able to discourage or prevent offensive—even better, questionable—situations from occurring. Whatever the form, education should encourage members to tell someone in their university Greek affairs office about any and all offensive incidents, and, of course, perpetrators should be punished accordingly.

Colleges could also scrutinize annual Greek events and restrict houses from holding any contests, games, or other events that appear sexist. Just as repercussions for sexual discrimina-tion and harassment in the workplace are enforced, so too should they be enforced on college campuses. Along the same lines, sexist attitudes might also be lessened if Greek advisors create new, healthier, and more respectful ways for Greek men and women to interact with one another. Coed events, volunteer service, open discussions, and educational programming can all help men and women achieve a better understanding of each other. For example, fraternities and sororities can participate in Adopt-A-School, a new program that focuses on service learning. Such a community-service project helps not only the young students at an adopted school, but also fraternity and sorority members, who are given an opportunity to work together.

Adopting a radical approach, faculty at Bucknell University in Lewisburg, Pennsylvania voted in 1989 to abolish single-sex fraternities and sororities, claiming they promote "racism, sexism, elitism, and anti-intellectualism."[19] And in January 1990, trustees at Vermont's Middlebury College announced that single-sex social organizations were antithetical to the objectives of the college, and ordered fraternities and sororities to become coed or face elimination. That spring, many of Sigma Epsilon's male members were skeptical when they pledged sixteen women to comply with Middlebury's new coed policy, but afterward, members were enthusiastic about the change; even excited about the new gender awareness they claimed to be cultivating. Since 1990, coed fraternities have appeared at several other colleges, including Bowdoin College in Brunswick, Maine, and Wesleyan College in Middletown Connecticut.[20]

In an interview with *Time* magazine, Michael Gordon, Executive Director of National Panhellenic Council at Indiana University in Bloomington, said that he believes coed policies will continue to spread to other campuses. "We are heading toward a whole new understanding of what a fraternity is," he said. "First they were seen as literary gatherings, then drinking clubs. What they will be in the future is living-learning centers."[21]

Indeed, it seems this recent move toward coed fraternities is a positive one. By placing men and women on an equal footing there is a greater chance of positive growth, for both sexes. Most members of the National Interfraternity Conference and National Panhellenic Conference disagree, however, claiming there are still good reasons to have single-gender organizations, especially for women. Arguably, women in a coed fraternity may miss out on some opportunities—namely, positions of leadership, as men historically have sought such posts and women have acquiesced. But just as women have gained and continue to gain ground in business, political, and other social arenas, with time, women will likely overcome such role stereotyping within a coed Greek system.

As with any profound, structural transformation, slow is the speed at which the Greek system is acknowledging and addressing sexism and sexual harassment. And just as all change begins with individuals, so, too, must individual fraternity and sorority members begin this journey. If Greek members were convinced that respecting the opposite sex is essential, sexism and sexual harassment might be distant memories.

Rather than perpetuating the sexist atmosphere so pervasive in Greek fraternities today, pressure to conform can be applied to reversing this damaging mindset. A former fraternity member explained that while he was an active he felt like a puppet with no control over his actions. "I guess I knew if I did not do and say things like my brothers, I would be made fun of, so I would find myself doing things I would have normally never done." He said that most men's attitudes are healthy when they first arrive at college, but are negatively influenced by being with a group of guys who belittle, insult, and have little—if any—regard for women. But if the attitudes of active members are changed for the better, then gradually as new pledges arrive, healthy attitudes will become the norm.

The more members that stand up for what is right, the more comfortable others will feel not participating in inappropriate or harmful situations. Such was the case for a friend who continuously refused to participate in his fraternity's routine ritual of performing sexual acts with strippers. "I was never really into being popular, but I always had a group of friends. I was not concerned about what people thought about me, so sometimes I would refuse to do what everyone else was doing, especially when everyone was just trying to outdo each other." At first, fellow members would heckle him, but after a few times of refusing he was left alone; soon, some of his friends decided not to participate, either. The bottom line is, it is always more respectable to do what is right, even if you are the only one, he said.

3
RAPE

The fraternity party was slowly dwindling in size. Two sorority sisters and I were ready to leave, but we couldn't find our assigned Little Sisters—new pledges we were to befriend over the semester. Knowing they wouldn't leave the party without us, we searched all over the downstairs of the fraternity house where the party was being held. No one knew where they were.

"Let's check upstairs," Stephanie suggested. My heart sank. There were only small bedrooms upstairs, mostly with locked doors. If they were inside, it would be difficult to find them, and it could mean bad news.

Reaching the top of the stairs, we saw a group of five familiar guys with their backs toward us, whispering together in front of one of the bedroom doors.

"Hi, guys, what's up?" I startled them.

"Uh . . . nothing," one answered hesitantly.

"Yeah," another chimed in, nervously. "We're just hanging out up here."

"Is anyone in that room?" I pointed to the door they were blocking.

"No, there hasn't been anyone up here for a long time."

"How would we know?" said another. "See, it's locked." He tried to turn the handle to demonstrate.

"Let me see." Stephanie pushed through them to the door and tried to open it without success. She knocked loudly. "Is anyone in there? Angela, Tiffany, Amanda—are you in there?"

The guys grew more and more agitated, trying to convince us to leave. My sorority sisters gave me skeptical glances—we knew all too well what might be going on. Each of us knew of more than one woman who had naively agreed to have "a few drinks" alone in a fraternity bedroom. The rule was, once a woman had passed out she was open game for sexual assault.

Panicked, I had an idea. The fraternity president was a friend of mine. "Wait here," I told my friends. "I'll go find the president." I hurried downstairs and finally convinced him to use the master key to open the door. After a few shouts of warning that we were coming, he swung the door open.

I felt ill as the smell of alcohol filled my nostrils. Spread out half-naked on the small beds were our three Little Sisters, passed out. Two fraternity members were frantically zipping up their pants.

"Here they are," the president said, unaffected by the scene. He smiled, pleased with himself for being so helpful. Then he left.

The two fraternity brothers started laughing and joking about what had been going on.

"You three really know how to ruin a party! Get this ho' off my bed," one brother said, trying to shove one of the women onto the floor.

"You guys are sick!" I said, shaking my head.

"How could you do this?" Stephanie asked, almost in tears.

"Relax, Stephanie," the other guy said. "You know they deserved it! They wanted it!" He slipped a T-shirt over his head and began calmly running a brush through his hair. They felt no remorse.

We began shaking our Little Sisters, trying frantically to

wake them. They were inebriated. After a few moments they woke up, but as we tried to pull them off the bed they flopped around, trying to lie back down. They were missing certain important pieces of clothing, which we helped them retrieve. Finally, some of our sorority sisters helped us carry them back to our house.

I'd often heard fraternity members talking about women they had gang-raped, but this was the first time I had actually broken up one of these sessions involving my own friends. I wish I could say that my friends and I took action against the sex offenders, but we didn't. We all knew it was rape, yet we kept quiet for fear of losing our social ties. We were engulfed in the Greek system, and well accustomed to the unspoken rules of the fraternity house.

Besides, I rationalized, my boyfriend was in that fraternity, and I'd spent several years building my social circle solely within that group. Not all of the brothers would approve of what happened, certainly, but I knew all would be penalized and angry if I reported it. To report their actions meant becoming a social outcast on campus.

What's more, the penalties they'd receive would be little more than a slap on the wrist. Just one semester before, the same fraternity had been put on probation for another gang rape—they were simply denied participation in rush and not allowed to hold parties during that semester. Meanwhile, the victim ended up leaving school, and took no legal action.

The day after the incident, our three Little Sisters had no memory of it, apart from being taken home. When we told them what had happened, they were embarrassed, and avoided parties at that fraternity from then on. Perhaps they, too, felt obligated to keep quiet.

This story may sound shocking, but gradually I learned that in my sorority and Little Sister program alone, at least half of my women friends had been raped. Most of them had been attacked by a single fraternity member who had lured them into a secluded area and forced himself on them, but some had also been raped by several fraternity men.

It has become apparent that fraternities are hotbeds of sexual violence. Gang rape, date rape, acquaintance rape, and battery are frequently committed upon many women who associate with fraternity members. According to Peggy Reeves Sanday in her book *Fraternity Gang Rape,* one fraternity had a designated rape room, and others included rape as part of the rite of initiation.[1]

On college campuses, at least one out of four women will be sexually assaulted, and 80 percent of the time the attackers will be fellow students.[2] According to research by clinical psychologists Stacey Copenhaver and Elizabeth Grauerholz, as well as other studies, these rapes will likely take place in a fraternity house and will be perpetrated by fraternity brothers.[3] A study done by the dean's office at the University of Illinois at Urbana-Champaign found that fraternity members, constituting one-fourth of the male students, were responsible for 63 percent of all sexual assaults reported at the university.[4]

GANG RAPE: A FRATERNITY RITUAL

There is much evidence that fraternities actively promote and participate in this most heinous sexual aggression called gang rape. One study sponsored by the Association of American Colleges found that fifty gang rapes occurred in fraternity houses across the country in a two-year period.[5]

Gary Tash, an alumnus and trial attorney, wrote in his fraternity's magazine that more than 90 percent of all gang rapes at colleges involve fraternity men.[6] The scene is usually similar to that with our Little Sisters, who were raped in a fraternity bedroom as several guys stood guard and awaited their turn.

A fraternity member explained that they are able to rape so many women by serving fruity drinks mixed with strong, but tasteless, alcohol. "The goal is to get them so drunk that they pass out, and wake up the next morning unsure if someone had sex with them the night before," he said, adding that the most important task for fraternity pledges was to be sure there were always plenty of drinks for the women at their parties.

According to a study conducted by Julie K. Ehrhart and Bernice R. Sandler "many fraternities glorify drinking and may deliberately encourage women to overdrink."[7] A 1990 study by M. E. O'Shaughnessey and C. Palmer proposes that victims of rape who had been drinking before the rape happened, particularly those under the age of twenty-one, had done so at fraternities.[8] Clearly, a strong link exists between the use of alcohol and rape, which partially explains how sexual assault has become so prevalent at fraternities.[9]

Current research also shows that in most cases, both the victims (79 percent) and their attackers (71 percent) were on drugs or alcohol around the time of the incident.[10] Dr. Clare Walsh, of the University of Florida's sexual-assault recovery program, said that most men don't realize it's illegal to have any sexual contact with a woman too drunk to be capable of giving permission.[11]

As one brother confided, fraternity members usually select someone at a party who is unaware of the routine, then try to get her into a bedroom to drink to the point of being unconscious. This is more often a new sorority pledge or Little Sister than a woman who has been around a while. My Little Sisters might not have gone upstairs with the fraternity members if they had been warned that it was dangerous territory and not an innocent extension of the party downstairs.

Fraternity members call the first few weeks of school "the honeymoon period" because new women are unaware how prevalent rape is at the fraternity houses.[12] Fraternity brothers will try anything—from flattery to subtle threats—to successfully persuade a woman to go somewhere private with them.

Kathleen Hirsch wrote in *Ms.* magazine that a woman is often led to a fraternity room under the impression that she will be with only one man or left alone to sober up. Instead, members are waiting to attack her in the room, or she wakes up while being raped by several men.[13]

WOMEN BEWARE

It seems that if a woman doesn't know how routinely rape occurs at fraternities, most of the time she automatically trusts the fraternity brothers. Oftentimes a woman will assume that because fraternity members are popular they will not hurt anyone. She may also feel comfortable with them because she has probably spent time getting to know them.

One sorority member told me she was raped by a fraternity member she had talked to frequently at parties, never imagining he could be violent. He was conservative and popular, not only in the Greek system, but with the college administration; friends had also told her he was a nice guy.

So she was taken completely by surprise by what happened after they'd had a few drinks and went to the fraternity's weight room.

"He pushed me down hard to the ground, sat his huge, heavy body tight on me, and roughly pulled down my pants. I remember yelling at him to stop, and fighting to get him off, but he was too strong. He raped me while I was crying, then said, 'This never happened.'"

Like this victim, most women know their offenders. According to a recent study of sorority women who had fallen victim to sexual force, an overwhelming proportion of women (95 percent) knew the men who assaulted them. In fact, 50 percent were sexually assaulted by men they were dating, 35 percent were assaulted by men they knew, and 10 percent were assaulted by male friends. The women in the study also reported that more than half (57 percent) of these rapes or attempted rapes occurred at a fraternity event or by a fraternity member.

Women—especially those unfamiliar with fraternities—beware. Studies prove fraternities breed rapists by encouraging and rewarding members who use sexual force on women.[14] Most researchers agree that a combination of conditions make fraternities especially dangerous for rapes and attempted rapes. Excessive use of alcohol, virtually no external supervision, support of violence, intense competition, and an overwhelmingly sexist atmosphere—including the extreme sexual objectification of women and widely encouraged use of pornography—all create an environment where sexual force is commended.

Two Florida State University Sociologists, Patricia Yancey Martin and Robert A. Hummer agree. In a recent study, they found that these kinds of conditions, coupled with a shared loyalty to protect the secrets of the group, create a culture where the use of sexual force is considered normal. Fraternities encourage rape because of the type of group they are, the members they have, the practices they participate in, and the absence of supervision, they report.[15]

From these studies it appears that women affiliated with the Greek system are at a higher risk of experiencing sexual force because it's encouraged within the Greek system. A 1991 study provides evidence that almost half of sorority women have experienced some kind of sexual coercion; 24 percent have escaped an attempted rape, and 17 percent have been raped. These percentages are consistent with a study that found sorority women were at greater risk of sexual assault than those who were not in a sorority.[16]

Women who are members of the Greek system are at a higher risk simply because they spend more time with fraternity members, according to Copenhaver and Grauerholz. Date parties, exchange parties, barbecues, annual events, rush parties, and other events provide more chances for sexual force to occur.[17]

Sorority members are also more likely to experience abuse in dating relationships than non-Greeks. Researchers recently found that 22 percent of college students have either received or inflicted physical abuse while in a relationship with another student. This same study reported that of those who had been abused, 50 percent were affiliated with a fraternity or a sorority. Of those who had never been in a violent relationship, only 8 percent were members of the Greek system.[18]

RAPES RARELY REPORTED

Far more rapes occur in fraternity houses than are ever reported or publicized. In her book, *I Never Called It Rape,* Robin Warshaw suggests that because women so rarely tell anyone about the attack, rapists consider them "safe" victims.

In a study of sorority members, researchers found that of those who had been raped, only a few reported it to police (2 percent), a rape crisis center (5 percent), medical officials (7 percent), parents (10 percent), or relatives (7 percent), and no one reported it to school officials. Within this sample, almost one-third told no one about what had happened to them.[19]

Many women won't tell anyone they were raped for the same reasons I didn't report the rape of our Little Sisters: fear of losing friends and facing harassment from other Greek members.

Gail Beyer, who worked as a Greek advisor at Ball State University in Indiana, said one woman didn't report being raped at a fraternity party because sorority sisters told her to drop it. "They told her they weren't going to pursue it because the fraternity wouldn't want to party with them anymore. They said the fraternity brothers would hate them."[20]

Overcoming harassment from fraternity members and becoming a school spectacle can be even more difficult than losing friends. If the victim does decide to report the crime, it doesn't take long before the entire fraternity knows who she is and tries to convince her to drop the charges.

One brother belonging to the same fraternity where our Little Sisters were raped explained that another woman who reported being gang raped eventually left school because the brothers and even some sorority sisters gave her such a hard time.

"Everyone was mad because we could not have any parties for a semester," he recounted. "If one of us ever saw her on campus, we would yell 'slut' or 'whore.'"

Ann Lane, founder of Colgate University's women's studies program, said that "most women feel that if they make a public statement they have to leave. They receive threats from fraternity brothers, and obscene phone calls. One woman got a rock thrown through her window."[21]

In addition, many rape victims are so traumatized by the experience that they have trouble paying attention in class, so their grades go down and they grow depressed and confused. This, along with harassment, causes many of the rape victims I've known personally to drop out of school, either for a semester or completely.

Another reason many rape victims don't report the incident is that they blame themselves instead of their attacker. As with many women in general, sorority women begin to believe the rape was their own fault. Such "rape myths" accuse the victim of wanting to be raped and perceive the behavior of the attacker as less violent. In fact, many women who believe these myths don't even realize they were raped, or, if they do, think the rape was their fault because they knew their assailant, they agreed to go to a secluded area with him, or they had been drinking.[22]

Along the same lines, many Greek women do not report rape because of their perceptions of male and female roles. As was discussed earlier, studies have proven that fraternity and sorority members believe strongly in traditional gender roles and therefore are more accepting of sexual force, rape, and physical abuse. Psychologists J. Garrett-Gooding and R. Senter, Jr., discovered that those who hold unhealthy views of sex roles not only accept the use of physical force, but are more likely to use it.[23]

Likewise, another study found that 44 percent of men who

held strong gender-role stereotypes had some chance of committing rape if assured of not being punished. However, only 12 percent of men who didn't have these stereotypes had some chance of committing rape if assured of not being punished.[24]

Based on my own experience, I believe that most fraternity and sorority members consider men superior to women. Within such a view, men are allowed to get away with abusive acts, simply because they can; it is almost acknowledged as their right. Even as a member in a sorority of seventy women, I always felt I belonged to a completely patriarchal organization. I frequently witnessed, heard about, or even suffered abuse (both physical and mental), attempted rapes, acquaintance rapes, and gang rapes.

LACK OF ADMINISTRATIVE SUPPORT

Victims who do decide to report a sex crime to their school usually find they receive little, if any, support from its administrators.

"It's a syndrome. We hear this over and over again," said Jeffrey Newman, an expert on sexual assault on college campuses and an attorney for a college rape victim. Interviewed by Kathleen Hirsch in *Ms.*, Newman stated, "The clinic head usually sends them to the school administration. The administration usually meets with the parents, probably with the school attorney present, to explain the benefits of undergoing the judicial process within the school, as opposed to the outside."

"What they're trying to do is intimidate the young woman into backing off," said Rosanne Zuffante, Newman's associate, in the same article. "And they succeed most of the time." They persuade the victims to report the crime only within the university, not to take legal action.[25]

Once a woman agrees, the rape case is handled internally in the university. The judicial board—a group of faculty and students established to review cases of plagiarism, vandalism, and the like—decides if the accused are guilty, and if they are, how they should be punished.

Critics argue that faculty, and especially fraternity and student members, on these boards are not qualified to examine rape charges. As Robin Warshaw pointed out, "It's ludicrous to assume that if a student is murdered by another student that the university would handle the investigation, and yet they see it as totally appropriate with rape."[26]

According to a 1991 survey by Towson State University Center, fewer than four in ten allegations of date rape result in any institutional penalties. Nevertheless, rape victims on campus often prefer the greater privacy and speed of university investigations.[27]

When perpetrators are punished, the consequence for rape is the same as, or less than, that for plagiarism: a year's suspension from school. Often the rapists don't even have to leave campus.

"It's a political game," attorney Newman said. "Usually there are strong connections between the D.A.'s office and the higher-ups in the university. Most of the time you find D.A.s drop the case or they never take it. They say, 'Look, there's just not enough evidence.'"

All too often, universities ignore rape victims in an effort to avoid the adverse publicity. These crimes are referred to as "isolated incidents" or "rare occurrences" on campus, "to keep consumers [students and their parents] and donors [alumni] ignorant and happy."[28]

AN ONGOING BATTLE

Colleges can no longer deny that rape is a serious problem on campuses and within the Greek system. Educating Greek students about the definition of rape and rape prevention is the first step toward change. The National Interfraternity Conference and National Sorority Conference now recommend that fraternities and sororities offer annual risk-management programs for their new members. Generally, individual fraternities and sororities, the university, or both, offer these programs in conjunction with local rape and crisis centers, and provide presentations, videos, and printed materials to educate participants about risk reduction and help them understand what are appropriate attitudes and actions.

As early as 1988, the National Interfraternity Conference started a commission on values and ethics that generated a variety of materials addressing topics such as rape. Some of the resultant case studies allowed fraternity and sorority members to discuss their feelings, attitudes, and possible reactions toward sexual promiscuity and unethical interactions between men and women. Seemingly, this kind of group discussion helps students mature without having to experience such negative situations personally. And about six years ago, the National Interfraternity Conference held the first International Conference of Sexual Assault, an annual meeting of university and fraternity professionals responsible for rape awareness and training. Jonathan Brant, the Executive Vice President of the National Interfraternity Conference, stated that the conference has created educational materials to help teach students and to address the following issues regarding sexual assault and harassment.

1. How to reduce sexual assault and harassment.
2. Ways to meet the needs of survivors.
3. Policy development and implementation.
4. Judicial and legislative concerns.
5. Security enforcement issues.

"From a Greek standpoint, we probably provide more education and programming for our Greek members than what other students might get," said an advisor of the National Panhellenic Conference. "Universities have resources, but if you are one student in a university of twenty-five thousand, do you really go out of your way to get the resource? If you are one student in a sorority house of one hundred members, you have the resource right there."

While I was a student, my own college took what I now consider positive steps toward preventing the opportunity for rape. College administrators ruled that no women would be allowed upstairs in fraternity houses on weekend nights, usually when parties and heavy drinking were occurring. They also put a twelve o'clock curfew on fraternity parties.

Rape is a serious issue, one that should concern Greek organizations enough to require their members to attend educational programming every semester. But universities' Greek councils also have the power to address sexual aggression on campus. For example, they can place restrictions on fraternity and sorority houses, like my own college did. And they can deter rape by encouraging victims to report sexual crimes to police, rather than the university.

SENSIBLE ADVICE FOR POTENTIAL VICTIMS

It is important to remember that rape can happen to anyone; therefore, it is crucial to be cautious and act responsibly always. Female students would be wise to use the "buddy system," staying close to or periodically checking in with a friend, especially while attending fraternity parties. Avoid drinking and taking drugs; these substances can severely diminish your capacity to make responsible decisions and drastically alter your behavior. If you do end up drinking or using drugs, however, know your limit and stop before you lose control.

If you do find yourself in a questionable situation, get out as soon as you can, even if you have to use physical force. If, after you have made every effort to escape, you are still attacked or raped, report the incident immediately. The best way to protect yourself and others from being raped by the same perpetrator is to go directly to your personal doctor or clinic (if you can avoid a college doctor) and have a rape kit performed. Never assume your college will take charge of bringing the perpetrator(s) to justice. Always, always, always file a report with the police. It is also a good idea to seek help from a local rape or crisis center, where staff is trained to deal with victims of violence and sexual aggression.

A WARNING TO POTENTIAL ATTACKERS

You may think that you would never be involved with rape, but it is shocking what some men will do to impress their fraternity brothers. Oftentimes fraternity members become so obsessed with being popular or fitting in that they stop thinking clearly. If your friends pressure you to commit rape, or even participate passively, they are not your friends. If you have reached the point of considering such an act, you have lost rational perspective. Take some time to regroup, away from your fraternal environment.

Many times men justify rape by claiming that the woman seemed to want sex. Perhaps it was the way she was dressed, or her actions. Perhaps men still believe that "no" really means "yes." Quite simply, rape is a serious and cruel crime. No one deserves it. And despite depictions to the contrary that—amazingly—continue to flood the media, no woman wants it.

If all else fails, think of yourself. Nothing is worth injuring another human being, committing a crime, and potentially losing your future. Realize that the consequence for committing rape could drastically alter your life forever. And while it is difficult to decline when you are surrounded by fraternity brothers who expect you to join them, it would be much less humiliating to refuse now than to get caught—and have to explain your actions—later.

4
DRUGS AND ALCOHOL

One hot, sunny day in Palm Springs, California, I was with hundreds of Greeks at a large hotel during our annual spring event. The partying had begun at ten in the morning, and I was now lying by the pool with a few of my friends. Although it was only early evening, many from our group had passed out on lawn chairs all around the pool. Several small accidents had already necessitated trips to the hospital for stitches or whatever—a common occurrence at Greek parties—but I wasn't prepared for what happened next.

It seemed like a long time since one of my friends had gone inside to the bathroom, so I decided to look for her. After roaming the halls of the hotel, I finally found her in an upstairs room with about ten other Greeks. It didn't take me long to realize what they were doing.

"Esther, wanna snort some coke?" my friend asked with a grin.

I shook my head, explaining that I wanted to go back to the pool with the others. Coke had never been my thing.

I had just settled back into my lawn chair by the pool when I looked up to see some people climbing from the hotel balcony to the roof. Gradually I recognized some of the same people I'd just left snorting cocaine. Hamming it up, one of the guys jumped off the roof into the pool below.

Obviously aware of the attention of those around the pool, the next guy walked to the edge of the roof. With a flourish, he turned around and pulled down his trunks, flashing his bare bottom to the crowd. As everyone laughed, he quickly pulled up his trunks and splashed into the water.

Two or three more guys took their turns jumping, also showing off for the crowd. Then I noticed one guy wobbling out to the edge of the roof. It was obvious he was out of control.

He tried to get a running start, but started off too slowly. Just as he reached the edge, he tripped, plunging toward the pavement below.

I stood up and screamed as he crashed onto a woman lying on a lawn chair not far from me. The ambulance was called, and both of them wound up in the hospital.

We later learned the guy jammed his toe so hard into the cement that doctors were unable to salvage part of it—to this day he only has half a toe. Likewise, the woman continues to suffer with permanent neck and back injuries. Rather than sue the fraternity, as she had planned, she settled out of court.

This story is a glaring example—albeit unfortunate—of what can happen when partying turns excessive, as it often does at fraternity parties. Drugs and alcohol are so prevalent that people often get hurt, sometimes with serious consequences. The guy in this story is actually luckier than was a twenty-year-old fraternity member at Pennsylvania's York College. When the drinking and partying got out of hand at his fraternity party, he fell off a building and died.

In this chapter we will examine how drinking and drug abuse are an integral part of college life, especially in the Greek system.

COLLEGE DRINKING:
A MONUMENTAL PROBLEM

Across the country, drinking on college campuses is the norm. Studies have found that as a group, college students drink more often and consume more alcohol per drinking incident than any other group of people in the United States.[1]

College-age drinking has been around for a long, long time, typically deemed a normal phase of becoming an adult and a customary part of the total college experience. But it can be defended no longer. Studies show that college students drink more today than in the past. In fact, according to Lisa Laitman, director of the Alcohol and Other Drug Assistance program at Rutgers University, 90 percent of today's college students drink.[2] A study by the Commission on Substance Abuse at Colleges and Universities, in Washington, D.C., comparing college drinking behavior between 1977 and 1989 reported that students at the end of the study got drunk more often than those at the beginning, and were more likely to drink to get drunk.[3]

"We have found that there are more people interested in drinking to get drunk," said Pam Bischoff, vice president for student affairs at Ramapo College in New Jersey. But "the real concern is that drinking leads to other kinds of problems."[4]

The Commission on Substance Abuse at Colleges and Universities, in Washington, D.C., found that one in three women surveyed said they drink solely to get drunk, up from one in ten in 1977.[5]

Likewise, a survey of 17,592 students on 140 campuses nationwide, the results of which were published in *The Journal of the American Medical Association,* found that in the two weeks preceding the survey 44 percent of college students had five or more drinks in a row on one or more occasions.[6] These students fit the definition of binge drinkers as described by the University of Michigan's Monitoring the Future Project.[7]

Students who indulge in binge drinking were found to be seven times as likely to have unprotected sex as non-binge drinkers. They were also found to be ten times as likely to drive after drinking, and eleven times as likely to fall behind in school.[8]

As bad as these statistics on college drinking are, some of the heaviest, most frequent, and most problematic drinkers on college campuses can be found in fraternities and sororities. Beer distributors alone spend an estimated $15 million a year advertising to college students, according to *USA Today*. Most of that advertising is directed at fraternities and sororities.

Greek students drink quite a bit more than non-Greeks. According to the Commission on Substance Abuse at Colleges and Universities, students that belong to a sorority or fraternity consume fifteen drinks a week, compared to an average of five for other students.[9] Fraternity and sorority members undoubtedly prefer alcohol as their drug of choice.

A study showed that during a thirty-day period, 98 percent of the Greeks drank some amount of alcohol every week, while only 47 percent used marijuana or cocaine.[10] Another study reported that 75 percent had used alcohol the week preceding the survey.[11]

It has also been reported that Greek students are less likely to perceive risk associated with drinking than non-Greeks. For example, research shows there is a significant difference between Greeks and non-Greeks in regard to having responsible drinking attitudes. Greeks are more likely to believe it's all right to drive after having a few drinks, and that "a real man" should be able to hold his liquor. Such inaccurate and irresponsible perceptions lead Greek members to drink more, which in turn causes them to have a significantly higher amount of alcohol-related problems than non-Greeks.[12]

A CULTURE OF DRUGS AND ALCOHOL

It is almost impossible to be in the Greek system and not drink alcohol or take drugs; it's embedded in the culture. While I was in college, I cannot remember meeting a single Greek student who was not an avid drinker.

The Greek system's reputation for the misuse of alcohol and drugs is well justified, thereby drawing members who have that activity in mind. Sororities and fraternities revolve around parties. In fact, based on research and my own experience, the constant availability of alcohol and drugs, especially for minors, is why many students join the Greek system in the first place. These are social organizations, first and foremost, and their parties unequivocally consist of students who are doing drugs, drinking alcohol, or both.

In my experience, the pressure to consume alcohol at fraternity and sorority parties is enormous. If a student dares not to join in the drinking festivities, he or she risks being the only sober person among thirty to a thousand drunks—a miserable situation in itself. What's more, a sober student will usually fall under close scrutiny by Greek partygoers. I know, because on rare occasions I was in that position.

At one such party, I couldn't drink because I was scheduled for surgery the next day. Most of the night, I was asked to explain why I wasn't drinking—unless there is a good excuse, those drinking are bothered when someone isn't joining them, and they have no qualms about letting you know it.

Throughout the night, I witnessed people yelling at the top of their lungs simply to say "hi" to each other. My fellow Greek members leaned on me for support, fell on me, kissed me, and spilled drinks all over me. One even vomited on me. It was not my idea of a good time. At previous parties, I had also been drinking and was just as sloppy as everyone else, so I never realized—until this particular party—how out of control the group was.

Drug and alcohol abuse has become so intertwined with Greek life that it is now one of the foundations of all their activities. These social organizations encourage drinking and drug use to excess, evidenced by Greek students' basic assumptions about life, not to mention their beliefs, values, and perspectives. Substance abuse is applauded and encouraged through the allocation of funds, organized drinking games, party-friendly decor, and rearranged class schedules, but most especially, the parties.

PARTY TIME

Though the shades were drawn, a tiny stream of light slipped into my darkened room, sending throbbing pain through my head. Shivering, yet sweating, I bundled the blankets tighter around me, wishing I could go to sleep. But every time I started to drift off, the dry heaves began again, as they had done all night. Now my stomach ached.

Each time the retching began, I tried to aim my vomit into a plastic bucket at the edge of my bed, but half of it always seemed to land on the side of my mouth, in my hair, on my comforter, and on my sheets. I was a miserable mess.

I knew I would have to miss a few days of school to get over such a severe hangover. Lying there, I tried to piece together what happened the night before to bring me to this state.

I clearly remembered being handed two large cups, one for each hand, as soon as I arrived at the fraternity party.

"Have another mimosa!" my fraternity friend insisted over and over throughout the night. I remembered laughing and drinking with him, but what so entertained us, as well as what happened afterward, escaped my memory. I later learned my roommates had to literally carry me home, because I fell on my face every time they put me down to walk.

Now, the grotesque, acidic smell of the room motivated me to empty my bucket. I tried to stand up, my knees wobbling beneath me. As I headed down the hall for the bathroom sink, the motion created a tidal wave in my stomach. After creating a few unexpected trails of vomit, I decided to return to my bedroom before one of my sorority sisters made me scrub it up. I was in no condition for cleaning.

Despite the way I was feeling, however, I knew it wouldn't be long before I was out partying again with the rest of them—though I vowed I would be a bit more careful. I was just like all the other Greeks—willing to sacrifice classes, grades, even physical comfort for a few hours of hearty partying. After all, in the Greek system, parties are the priority.

Greeks plan and attend an amazingly large number of parties each semester, consuming much of their free time in college. Besides rush parties, there are pledge and initiation parties, football parties that begin at 10 A.M. and last into the night, at least five theme parties per semester held jointly by sororities and fraternities, annual event parties lasting an entire week, formals, date parties, and couples' pinning parties—the list goes on and on.

In addition to all these parties, there are sports competitions and organized weekend and holiday trips to Lake Tahoe, Las Vegas, Mexico, and other favorite party spots—they all serve as a reason to party.

At the center of each of these events is drug use and drinking to excess. A sorority member referring to the Greek system said it best: "I think without alcohol, parties would be nonexistent."[13]

Most Greeks wouldn't dream of missing any of these events. In fact, they usually put partying before academics. Most will try to arrange their schedules so parties and expected hangovers won't coincide with their classes. I found that if Greek students couldn't arrange a schedule that left them free to party, they would usually miss a class occasionally, or not even sign up for the conflicting class in the first place.

For example, most Greeks avoid scheduling classes on Fridays, because there are always as many—and sometimes more—parties on Thursday nights as on weekend nights. After a hard night of partying, it's especially difficult to get up the next morning. Usually Greeks don't get up until Friday afternoon, just in time to get ready for the next party. From my experience, most Greeks avoid morning classes as well, because important parties may be held any night except Sunday.

"Hangover" is daily part of speech among Greeks; it is the most popular excuse for missing classes or not doing homework.

If I had put the same effort into my classes as I put into attending parties, I would have soon earned a full scholarship to a university, and would now be working on a doctorate degree. But as it turned out, my sorority sisters and I spent too many mornings in bed on school days, amazed that we even survived the night before.

There is no question that drinking alcohol and taking drugs reduced our productivity, caused us to miss classes, and lowered our grades. And we're not alone. Research has proven that students who drink the most have lower grade-point averages.[14]

For many students, unfortunately, the habit of partying doesn't stop once they graduate from college. All too often, Greek members get so used to the pattern that they develop a full-blown drug or alcohol dependency.

Since my graduation in 1992, I've seen or heard that many of the Greeks I graduated with still maintain the habits they formed in college. They are working, but partying frequently takes priority over their careers. Instead of going to Greek parties, they frequent specific bars, getting drunk at least two or three times a week. It seems that four years of consistent conditioning in college have produced a dependency on these rituals, making it very difficult to stop. By definition, they are drug addicts, alcoholics, or both.

For example, one fraternity friend who started taking ecstasy at college parties still—two years later—takes it at least three times a week. Being addicted to ecstasy is extremely dangerous because it drains the liquid from the spine, causing individuals to lose control, strength, and sensitivity in their legs. In some cases, ecstasy users suddenly collapse because their legs give out on them without warning. An older fraternity member who sold ecstasy when I was a Little Sister cannot even walk now without the support of a cane.

As with any addiction, it is the frequent and regular use of drugs and alcohol that lead to dependency. For Greek members, that use frequently numbers at least three times a week.

MONEY DOWN THE BOTTLE

When Greeks are not playing drinking games themselves or forcing pledges to drink, they usually are financing parties where the alcohol flows freely. A fraternity social chairman estimated that his fraternity spent at least $30,000 each semester on alcohol, using almost all of their monthly membership fees.

The huge amounts of money poured into alcohol was also seen by researchers who studied four fraternities on two different campuses. The researchers reported that the subject fraternities traditionally used members' fees toward social events, including the purchase of alcohol.[15] No doubt, this is a common practice at most fraternities.

What is a lesser-known practice is using budget monies to supply drugs. Fraternity officials estimate such allocations occur about half of the time, and are usually listed as food or decoration expenses. During my own college years, I don't remember attending a single Greek party where marijuana and ecstasy weren't readily available. Usually at least one person sold drugs to the party guests, or the fraternity would simply give the drugs away.

DRINKING-FRIENDLY DECOR

The drinking symbols and decor displayed in most fraternity houses also reveal the degree to which drinking is imbedded within the Greek system. Most houses look similar to the inside of a bar, decorated with neon beer signs, "girlie" beer posters, and other alcoholic signs and symbols placed prominently throughout the common living space. Each house has a main bar, with additional bars in the larger bedrooms. Lots of bottles, shot glasses, and imported beers are usually on display. Furniture is inexpensive and spare, with the exception of pool tables; anything of value runs the risk of getting trashed.

GAMES OF EXCESS

Another custom at most Greek gatherings is organized drinking games. I have spent hours playing such drinking games as "quarters," "caps," and many others using cards. The penalties always involve taking a swig or guzzling some type of alcohol, often beer. Whoever has not passed out is the winner.

"Caps," or "caps till you puke," was particularly popular at the fraternity where I was a Little Sister. The object was to throw a bottle cap into a cup placed on the floor between the opponent's legs. If a cap makes it into the cup, the opponent must take a swig of beer.

This goes on until someone vomits. If the person licks up his own vomit, he can stay in the game—and most members do this to try to win. The person who has not passed out—and is willing to keep playing—is the winner.

Researchers have found that most college fraternities and sororities participate in drinking games like these, which encourage excessive drinking.

Such games may also be played with drugs. One fraternity member wrote a letter to his college administration describing the use of LSD, ecstasy, cocaine, and other drugs in his house. He recounted frightening games such as "drug olympics" between actives and pledges, and a "tequila night" during which a record was kept of shots consumed. The member who wrote the letter confessed to drinking thirty-three shots of tequila; the winner drank forty-three.[16]

Not surprisingly, drinking to this excess can result in alcohol poisoning. One example was described by a twenty-one-year-old fraternity pledge at Indiana University who nearly died during his initiation party.

First, the entire pledge class was ordered to strip down to their underwear, blindfolded, and paraded around the fraternity house while sorority members tugged on their shorts and wrote on their bodies with felt-tip markers. Next the pledges were forced to drink from "beer bongs"—large plastic funnels attached to plastic tubes through which beer is poured down the pledges' throats. When consumed in this manner, beer goes quickly to the head, causing someone to get drunk after only one "hit."

Once the pledges vomited, they were allowed to stop doing the bongs. For this particular pledge, however, it seemed no amount of beer could make him vomit. Finally, when he was the last pledge standing, they rewarded him with shots of whiskey until he fell face-first to the ground, blood gushing from his nose.

By the time he was taken to the hospital, the pledge was in a coma. His blood alcohol level was .48 (.50 is usually fatal), and he could hardly breathe. Luckily, he regained consciousness seven hours later, and lived to tell the tale.[17]

Not all participants are so lucky. James Callahan, an eighteen-year-old Rutgers University student, died of alcohol poisoning after drinking a combination of vodka, triple sec, and lime juice at a drinking marathon during his fraternity initiation.[18] Alcohol poisoning can happen to anyone, and it is serious. Unfortunately, Greeks rarely view it as such until it's too late.

A LETHAL MIX

When fraternity and sorority members drink or take drugs, they usually ignore the harmful effects and potentially fatal situations that could result. In previous chapters, some of the problems related to alcohol and drug use—such as hazing deaths, sexual harassment, and rape—have been addressed. Unfortunately, there are many others.

I personally have seen severe cases of alcohol poisoning, drug overdose, car accidents, and other types of accidents caused by members using drugs or drinking. Besides the illegal sale and use of drugs, I've seen members damage property on several occasions, and have also seen them suffer serious consequences from poor grades and lack of attendance in classes.

Alcohol is an addictive drug. It is a tranquilizer, or relaxant, not an energizer. Many Greeks rely on it to rid themselves of inhibitions, causing them to feel more creative and sometimes more aggressive. These alleged benefits are only temporary, however. A few hours after drinking, the blood sugar drops and they begin to feel weak, dizzy, confused, and abnormally hungry. The next day the drinker is left with a hangover, largely caused by severe and sudden dehydration of the body. At the very least, the result of excessive drinking is unpleasant; at most, it can be deadly. In addition to alcohol poisoning, excessive drinking— when done over a long period of time—can lead to alcoholism, a disease that wreaks havoc with its victim's physical and emotional well-being, not to mention those around him or her.

Marijuana is also, once again, becoming a drug of choice on campuses nationwide, making it more dangerous than ever. A 1994 survey at the University of Minnesota's Twin Cities campus found that 14 percent of students had smoked marijuana in the previous month, compared with 11 percent in 1989 and 6 percent in 1992. The survey found that among freshmen, marijuana use jumped from 8 percent in 1992 to 22 percent in 1994.[19]

While marijuana reportedly relaxes and heightens perception in its users, it also causes mood swings, lack of physical coordination, sluggishness, and sometimes nausea. Using marijuana over a long term has been shown to decrease motivation and damage the brain, heart, lungs, and reproductive system.

Besides alcohol and marijuana, a wide variety of other drugs will likely be offered to fraternity and sorority members. Each drug elicits potentially powerful effects, and can be dangerous because of the resultant altered states.

From my own experience, ecstasy and crystal methane are becoming increasingly popular among college students, along with psychedelics such as mushrooms and "acid," or LSD. These drugs are erratic, sometimes producing frightening hallucinations rather than pleasant ones. Some long-term effects of their use are brain damage, and liver and kidney malfunction.

Cocaine, or "coke," is another popular drug that excites the nervous system and produces intense sensations that can also be hallucinogenic. Sniffing the drug can create ulceration of nasal passages, itching, and open sores. Long-term use can also destroy the heart and lungs.

Amphetamines, or "uppers," and methamphetamines, or "speed," are also frequently used by Greek students, especially during midterms and finals, or to aid in weight loss. They are taken to speed up physical and mental processes, increasing users' energy and excitement. Some of the side effects are weight loss, insomnia, diarrhea, paranoia, violent behavior, and, in the event of an overdose, potential death.

Clearly, death by overdose is the most severe consequence of using drugs. But what many don't realize is that overdose can result not only from taking too much of a drug, but also from taking a drug too strong for the human body to tolerate. I saw both types personally.

I was standing in line at Disneyland with about twelve other Greek members when suddenly one of our friends jerked forward, his entire body crashing onto the pavement. About ten minutes earlier, he had eaten a large package of psychedelic mushrooms.

As I saw him lying stone-cold on the pavement, it seemed that time stood still. His sunglasses were broken and twisted against his face, blood gushing from his nose.

"Oh, my God, he's dead!" I shouted, my heart pounding with fright. Everyone crowded around him. He was so limp that it took six big fraternity brothers to lift him and carry him away to get help. I was filled with fear as I imagined the worst: Was he dead?

My friend survived, but he's never forgotten that day; he almost lost his life. Unfortunately, most Greeks thought it was funny when we told them about the experience. They were just like we had been before witnessing this scene; they couldn't even comprehend the grave danger of taking drugs.

Even if students don't do drugs, and declare their intention not to do so at a party, they may get more than they bargain for. All too often, fraternity brothers slip drugs into drinks being served at parties—especially into those of female guests—without anyone's knowledge, or consent. My roommates and many other friends had this happen to them a number of times.

Another common problem is "lacing," mixing a stronger drug with another. For example, if students agree to smoke marijuana, expecting a mild high, they may also end up smoking a stronger drug that was laced into the marijuana, and may experience hallucinations or other side effects for which they are unprepared. This, too, occurs frequently without students' knowledge or permission.

This happened to a friend while a member of a fraternity in California. At a fraternity party, he overdosed on PCP that had been laced in the marijuana someone gave him. For three years afterward, he suffered occasional flashbacks from this frightening experience. At the same party, another fraternity member became so intoxicated that he jumped off the roof and died. While less frequent than reports of alcohol-related accidents and alcohol poisoning, stories of tragic deaths resulting from involuntary drug abuse are all too common.

THE INHERENT RISKS

The frightening realities related to excessive use of alcohol and drugs have apparently not been recognized by many Greeks. Like most young people, Greek students tend to think their youth will protect them from the risks involved. Studies and the following examples—as well as hundreds of similar stories—indicate this assumption is simply not true.

ARRESTS
Besides the physical dangers, there is always the possibility that students who use and deal drugs could be arrested. Such acts are, after all, illegal.

At the parties I attended, clouds of smoke regularly poured out of the fraternity house when the windows were opened, and drug dealers freely passed around clear plastic bags of ecstasy pills. I never saw any fear or concern about getting caught.

During the same time, in Charlottesville, Virginia, a twenty-one-year-old student was found guilty of selling marijuana and hallucinogens from his fraternity bedroom, and faces up to ten years in prison. He and eleven of his fraternity brothers were arrested in one night for selling drugs to undercover agents.

Before the arrests, the fraternity members reportedly showed no fear of being caught. "Many a night a police officer would ride by [one of the houses], and they'd be in there smoking dope, and they'd laugh," recounted the twenty-three-year-old undercover agent. "They believed they were untouchable."[20]

Personally, I found that people outside the Greek system appeared to be much more cautious when using or selling drugs.

ACCIDENTS

Another dangerous, and possibly fatal, outcome of drinking or taking drugs springs forth when people drive under the influence. Indeed, a spokesperson from the United States National Highway Traffic and Safety Administration reported that alcohol is a factor in roughly half of all automobile accidents. Still, many Greeks are irresponsible when it comes to drinking and driving.

I have personally been in two alcohol-related car accidents in which the cars were totaled. The first time, I was riding with a group of drunk fraternity Little Sisters; the second, I was with a group of drunk sorority sisters. Fortunately, no one was seriously hurt in either instance, but had we been stopped, the drivers could have easily received citations for drunk driving.

Several other Greek members I know have received such citations. DWIs—or DUIs, as they are called in some states—are very expensive, usually requiring the offender to attend Alcoholics Anonymous meetings and to fulfill many hours of community service (often spent picking up trash beside the road). Such citations can remain on their record permanently, thus preventing them from pursuing certain careers, like the practice of law. And with organizations such as Mothers Against Drunk Driving (MADD) on the trail, punishments will likely become stiffer.

Many Greeks I've known have also been in accidents. One fraternity friend was so drunk that he totaled his car by running into a sign post on a concrete island in the middle of the road. He had to walk seven miles to get home, yet was so inebriated that the next morning he woke up wondering where his car was. He was fortunate not to have hit someone, especially since his driver's license had already been taken away. This accident earned him his third citation for drunk driving.

Several years ago, a drunk fraternity pledge at the University of Arizona was driving home from a fraternity party when he hit another car. The other driver, a business executive, was left blind, brain-damaged, and a quadriplegic. He later died. Court records report the pledge's blood alcohol level was .15 percent, more than 50 percent higher than the legal limit in most states.[21]

Some Greek students may argue that if they live on "Greek row," they don't have to drive after drinking at a party. Many colleges do have a "row" or street where all the fraternity and sorority houses are located, but this was not the case at the first university I attended. Fraternity and sorority houses were spread all over town, and the fraternity where I was a Little Sister was a fifteen-minute drive away from campus and the dorms. Yet I never saw a student call for a cab after a party, and I only heard the words "designated driver" when students mocked its purpose: "Oh no, was I the designated driver?" party goers would joke before guzzling consecutive shots in a contest.

The second university I attended did have a Greek row, and I did notice a decrease in the amount of drunk driving. However, many Greek members would still leave parties drunk to drive to an off-campus club, bar, or liquor store for more alcohol.

PROPERTY DAMAGE

Alcohol is known to produce aggressive and sometimes violent behavior, as many a member of a fraternity cleanup crew can attest. Fraternity parties are expected to end with a broken window or burned piece of furniture, at the least. Not surprisingly, a Greek advisor reported that fraternities are the third most risky properties to insure, only ranking behind toxic waste dumps and amusement parks.

In December 1995, a fire started in one of the fraternities at the University of Southern California. The fire was reported to have started in one room on the second floor, then traveled down the hallway and entered other rooms through open doors. As Ken Taylor, director of the Office of Residential and Greek Life at U.S.C., reported, not only did the house suffer damage but one fraternity member, Gary Douglas, suffered second and third-degree burns on his back and legs.

Investigators believe that some kind of incendiary device may have been the cause of the fire. Other sources who were there when the house caught fire report that some of the fraternity members, who had been drinking, decided to set off fire crackers and other explosives in the house. One of the explosives caught fire and quickly moved through the house.

Such damage can occur on both campus property as well as that of the surrounding community. Vandalizing university housing is a popular pastime for Greeks, who are often on hallucinogens as they spray-paint halls and bedrooms. I have seen drunken Greeks destroy cars and buildings that belong to non-Greeks and even nonstudents. Once, during a fraternity party, I saw a brother outside the house jumping on and denting parked cars. Recently, four fraternity pledges at California State University-Northridge even stole the historic marker bell from the San Fernando Mission.[22]

At times, drunken parties can incite near riots. In April 1995, as many as a thousand students at the University of Wisconsin-Oshkosh campus marched through the town in the early hours of the morning, breaking windows and tearing down traffic lights and signs after police raided a fraternity party. The police had issued 174 citations at the party—mostly for under-age drinking—causing the students to take to the streets. Twelve people were arrested for damaging between fifteen and twenty businesses.[23]

REGRET

Although many students may consider regret a risk milder than most, particularly those previously mentioned, embarrassing or humiliating images of earlier behavior and mistakes can last a lifetime. Drinking to excess causes people to do things they later regret. I've known many a Greek member who woke up "hating life" because of something he or she did under the influence— something all of them wish had never happened.

One sorority friend had a habit of getting into such situations. One time she was so drunk that she thought it was a good idea to go skinny-dipping in the university's fountain with a group of fraternity brothers—she being the only one with enough nerve to remove all her clothing. Consequently, she was the only one singled out by campus security officers, and was forced to "sleep it off" in their office. This incident and others earned her such a reputation on campus that she finally trans-ferred to another college.

THINK TODAY, PROTECT YOURSELF TOMORROW

For those involved in the Greek system, it is often hard to think about the possible, yet potentially serious, repercussions of using drugs and alcohol. Having left home—often for the first time of any length—students suddenly find themselves in a world with-out restrictions. From the time new students become pledges they are pressured to go to party after party and consume drink after drink. And so many others participate in this attempt at "getting wasted," it seems like the normal thing to do. What Greek students often forget, however, is that they are only a small group, within a much larger group of university students pursuing more serious conquests. While many Greek members are spending their time focusing on who can hold the most shots before puking, other students are getting an education and planning for their future.

If partying is important to you, do not fall into the trap of excess. It is for your own protection that you know your limits and do not go beyond them. Though most of those around you might be drunk, you are responsible for protecting yourself. After all, it is you who will live with the consequences. If you do something foolish or get hurt in an accident, you are damaging yourself, and you may endanger the lives of others. And, though rape is never the fault of the victim, it will be you who suffers— not to mention your future—if you put yourself in a position where you're out of control or have no knowledge of what is happening to you.

SETTING STANDARDS

The latest trend in combating excessive drinking is establishing "substance-free" housing for fraternities. Historically, most fraternities have been allowed alcohol with the assumption that the members were following national risk-reduction policies—not allowing underage drinking and otherwise drinking responsibly. Research has indicated, however, that students drink whether they are of age or not, and often act irresponsibly. Furthermore, such policies seem impractical, since most fraternity members are younger than legal drinking age—which in most states is twenty-one. Substance-free housing, which prohibits all alcohol from being used on the premises, period, seems a better solution.

A member of the National Interfraternity Conference said that today, some chapters require that all new fraternity houses be substance free. Reportedly, it is difficult to change an existing house because its members joined under certain circumstances, one of which is that they could use alcohol. Some fraternity houses are also becoming substance free voluntarily, or after a chapter is reorganized. Reorganization occurs when a house is closed and reopened, or when only a few members are allowed to remain with the chapter because of a violation.

Two of the earliest fraternities to become substance free were Sigma Chi at the University of Maine and Alpha Tao Omega at Indiana University, which now have about four years of sobriety under their belts. The entire campus at the University of Colorado fraternity system chose to become substance free in all Greek activities. Most recently, in the fall of 1995, the fraternity of Sigma Tao Gamma at the University of Illinois became substance free. National advisors say more chapters would become substance free if members were convinced they would still be able to enjoy themselves without alcohol.

National Interfraternity Conference member Jonathan Brant said there are probably only a couple dozen such fraternities in the country. "It is a win, win, win, situation if a chapter will become substance free," he said. "It does not mean we will eliminate the hazing, accidents, fighting, sexual assault, and other concerns, but it will certainly cut down on the possibility of them occurring."

Along the same lines, Greek houses at California State University-Long Beach have always been scattered throughout town, but now university officials have offered to establish a nonalcoholic Greek row. The row would fall under the classification of university housing, enabling officials to enforce alcohol restrictions. The University of Illinois has also prohibited alcohol at late-night fraternity parties, and most houses have a member on site who is prepared to advise and interrupt when a violent situation occurs. Some colleges, such as Rhodes College in Providence, Rhode Island, and Millsaps College in Jackson, Mississippi, have moved to nonresidential fraternities.

While these organizations have taken some positive steps,

however, such examples are few and far between. More often, administrators have given up hope, providing little, if any, supervision at most fraternity houses. Many fraternities have even begun to view alcohol and risk-management policies as a game, the goal being not to get caught. For example, Farm House fraternity claims to have never allowed alcohol in its chapters; nevertheless, most houses have always had alcohol on the premises.

What's more, educating college students about the risks of excessive drinking does not seem to be lessening consumption. "Students today could tell you anything you would like to know about alcohol; it doesn't necessarily change the way they consume it or do not consume it," a member of the National Interfraternity Conference explained. "If they have already decided that they are or are not going to drink, they seem to just continue their pattern. We have very knowable drinkers on campus, and, unfortunately, since alcohol is so central to other problems, it is not likely they [sexual harassment, hazing, racism, and sexism, rape, and so on] will be diminished."

In a presentation at the 1995 meeting of the National Interfraternity Conference, Dr. Michael Hanes from Northern Illinois University suggested a possible solution to students' ever increasing alcohol consumption. He described a perceptual study, conducted on his campus for the last four years, in which students were given questionnaires and asked, "What, and to what extent, do you think your fellow students are drinking? . . . sexually active? . . . studying?" Responses suggested that students believed other students were drinking all of the time. Then, students were instructed to answer the same questionnaire based on their own activities. The study proved that students' perceptions about the type and frequency of such activities were at a much higher level than reality.

The second part of the study consisted of students reading newspaper advertisements that cited actual statistics on their campus, in terms of drinking, sexual activity, and number of hours spent studying. Once students discovered that their fellow students weren't really drinking as much as was perceived, they did it less; as a result, binge drinking went down more than 34 percent. One possible explanation for this dramatic drop is students' overwhelming need to fit in.

To create a Greek system that parents and faculty can once again trust, on a national level, it will take more than a few houses making a some changes. It will take the entire organization agreeing and complying with an essential plan for change. Henry Wechsler, director of the Alcohol Studies Program at the Harvard School of Public Health, hit the target when he said that college administrators and students themselves must make drunkenness unacceptable.[24] Until we do, college students are risking not only their grades, but their health and possibly their entire futures.

5
RISKY SEX

My sorority sister's eyes were puffy, her face stained with tears.

"Esther, my life is ruined! I have gonorrhea." She buried her head in her pillow and began sobbing as I tried to be sympathetic.

"It's all Joe's fault," she continued. "I just slept with him one time, and look what happened. Now I probably gave it to my boyfriend, and he'll find out I was with Joe."

I knew she and Bill had been dating faithfully since high school, and this could only mean trouble in their relationship. The uncomfortable itching and burning were unmistakable—it was gonorrhea. And although the disease was treatable, it wouldn't go away easily.

"Are you sure Joe gave it to you?"

She nodded. "Yes. I know Bill wouldn't dream of sleeping around, so I asked Joe about it last night. He said he had gonorrhea a while ago, but thought he was over it. And I wasn't the only one—several other girls asked him about it last night, too.

"Oh, Esther, what am I going to do? I love Bill so much—and now I'm going to lose him!"

I tried to console her for the rest of the afternoon, counseling her through guilt and depression, and offering possible solutions. But my efforts didn't help.

A week later Bill called to confront her. He now had gonorrhea, and because he had been loyal to her for three years, she was the only one who could have given it to him. He felt so angry and betrayed that he flatly broke up with her. My friend pleaded humbly for Bill's forgiveness, but to no avail.

She spent the rest of the year trying to get him back, but nothing worked. He barely acknowledged her existence. If they did end up in the same room at a party, he wouldn't even look at her. She was devastated.

Every day, thirty-three thousand Americans become infected with a sexually transmitted disease. Because young people are generally more promiscuous, less likely to use condoms, and less likely to see a doctor, and because young women are more biologically susceptible to sexually transmitted diseases, they are the generation of Americans who stand to suffer the greatest consequences of these actions.[1]

Sex is considered "safe" between two individuals who are free of disease and who remain in a trustworthy, monogamous relationship—and even then, the risk of unwanted pregnancy remains. The next best option for safe sex is to use condoms, but they are not foolproof, either. Every year, 14 to 16 percent of women who use condoms get pregnant—a failure rate higher than that of the pill or an IUD. Condoms can also break or slip off, eliminating protection completely. The risk of a condom breaking is between 1 and 7 percent; the risk of a condom slipping off is between 1 percent and 6 percent.[2]

Clearly, then, the only true "safe sex" is abstinence. Such an alternative seems unacceptable in the Greek system, however; even monogamous dating is scorned. Casual dating and unprotected sex are the norm. In a study of college students, researchers found that dorm residents and students who live off campus were twice as apt not to date as those in the Greek system. Greek residents, meanwhile, were more likely to go out on dates twice a week or more.[3] From these statistics, it becomes apparent that Greeks are more likely to be involved in frequent casual dating than in committed, monogamous relationships. Thus, because frequent, casual dating often means frequent, casual sex—which is likely to be unprotected sex—members of fraternities and sororities are at the highest risk of catching a sexually transmitted disease or becoming pregnant.

In this chapter, we will examine how those in the Greek system promote such a casual attitude toward sex, and how that sexual activity puts them at higher risk for unwanted pregnancy, AIDS, and other sexually transmitted diseases.

GREEK PARTIES

The provocative and sexually charged atmosphere at fraternity and sorority parties has already been discussed. Ask any fraternity member the purpose of these parties, and he will mostly likely answer, "to get laid."

Many times, Greek parties serve merely as a vehicle for drinking and linking up with someone with whom to end the night in a bedroom. Actually, drinking is also a means toward that end. Some Greeks are so desperate to find a sex partner that they willingly allow themselves to put on what are commonly called "beer goggles." In other words, they drink so much that anyone who ends up in their bed looks sexy, even someone they would usually find unattractive.

Most Greeks believe that any sex is better than no sex at all, even if it's with someone they despise when they're sober. So, despite the horrifying "morning-after" stories I've heard so often, the ritual continues.

"You'll never believe who I slept with last night," a fraternity member confided after a long night of partying. "This ugly girl who I heard is the biggest slut on the row! She's just crawling with diseases! Did I have beer goggles on last night or what?"

87

Another fraternity friend also recounted a party when he wore "beer goggles."

"I had been drinking all night, so when some of the guys suggested I ask this girl to dance, I took them up on it. I guess we made a scene, because I still hear about it. The next morning I was shocked when I woke up next to this fat, heinous girl."

He said he was so embarrassed that he quickly got up, told the woman he was late for a hair appointment, and left before she was even out of his bed. He waited at a friend's house all day to be sure he wouldn't have to see her again. When he got back to the fraternity house, he learned she had waited for him until noon.

Just as embarrassed about their own drunken escapades, many of my sorority sisters tried to sneak away from their sex partners the morning after, only to find they were locked out of the sorority house without their key. Many a morning I would wake up to a sister standing outside my bedroom window, or that of another friend, calling for someone to let them into the house. Amazingly enough, this happened so often that fraternity and sorority members made an event of it, getting up "early" (which meant about ten) to heckle the parade of individuals returning to their houses, still wearing their clothes from the night before.

Parties are also the main organizing link for having multiple sexual partners. Scores of women—especially freshmen—are invited to fraternity parties, creating hundreds of opportunities to meet many potential sex partners; sororities organize similar parties, as well. In my own experience, I've found that many Greeks have multiple partners each week, or even each night. A "live-it-up" attitude is pervasive at fraternity parties, where members are encouraged to throw caution to the wind and have sex with whomever.[4]

I chose to remain faithful to my boyfriend during my entire time in college, and was constantly badgered for it by fraternity and sorority members who indulged in frequent sexual exchanges. Although I knew a few who chose to remain monogamous, we were a definite minority.

Parties are just one vehicle to hook up with a multitude of sexual partners, however. During my senior year, when I would stay in the sorority house to study on week nights, I often sat on the balcony and observed the mating ritual. At about 9:30 P.M., groups of three or four fraternity guys and groups of three or four sorority women would pass by on their way to the bar at the end of Greek row. Then, after the bar closed at 2:00 A.M., drunken couples would make the return trip, stumbling down the street, hanging all over each other, and anxiously awaiting sex.

VIRGINITY: A DIRTY WORD

I still remember the pain I felt when my first college crush—a fraternity brother—broke up with me when he realized I was still a virgin and didn't want to have sex with him. Not long after, I began dating another fraternity brother whom I really liked. Afraid of losing him as well, I felt I had no choice but to sleep with him.

Afterward, I overheard this guy bragging to his fraternity brothers—who all knew I was a virgin—about what we had done. I was the conquest he used to gain the respect of his brothers.

Thinking back, I heard many guys talk openly about virgins they knew in the Greek system. If the women were new, the brothers competed to be the first one to sleep with her. If she was still a virgin by her second year of college, she was labeled a prude.

The ultimate humiliation for a guy in the Greek system is to be a virgin himself; in fact, it would be nearly impossible to find one who would admit it. I certainly never knew any—or, if I did, I didn't know it at the time. In fraternities, sexual prowess is the supreme proof of manliness.

THE CONSEQUENCES

With such high stakes, it's unfortunate that Greeks don't tolerate those who choose abstinence. After all, abstaining from sex is the only way to completely protect oneself from unwanted pregnancy, genital warts and pubic lice, AIDS, and other sexually transmitted diseases.

PREGNANCY

I had followed the directions exactly, and now sat on my bed, waiting. It seemed like the longest five minutes of my life. How had I let this happen? I should have taken precautions. But with so many things on my mind during finals, I had forgotten to take the pill two days in a row. Now, my period was noticeably late, and I was worried. All I could do was wait while my future was to be determined by a drugstore pregnancy test.

I didn't want to have an abortion, though all my friends who had gotten pregnant had done so. I knew the procedure would end my anguish today, but it would haunt me the rest of my life. Maybe I could move home, drop out of college, and have the baby—if I could get up enough nerve to tell my parents, that is. But if I did that, would I have to put the baby up for adoption? And when it came time, could I give my baby away? Not being able to think anymore, I began crying uncontrollably.

I don't know how long I sobbed, but eventually I realized there was no way out. It was time to check the test.

Standing up, I went to my dresser, fearful, expecting the worst. To my relief, the test clearly showed I was not pregnant. In that moment, all my fears melted away, but I will never forget the horror I had felt.

A 1994 survey showed that of college students who are sexually active, 47 percent of men and 32 percent of women reported having sex without birth control, a practice that can only lead to unwanted pregnancies.[5] In my own sorority, I know of several women who got pregnant—in fact, four of my closest friends confided in me when they found out they were pregnant-

—although this kind of information was kept strictly confidential. I suspect there were many others as well.

Abortion was always the way out; during my college years, two of my friends had two abortions each, and the other two each had one abortion. They all felt guilty about their decision at the time, but for a variety of reasons—financial instability or the daunting task of raising a child alone—each tried to convince themselves that abortion was the best choice. I later learned that others still feel guilty, and wonder what their lives would have been like if they had chosen a different option.

When my roommate thought she might be pregnant, she used the quickest method of dealing with the situation by going to the college health center for a "morning-after" pill. Supposedly created for women to avoid the agony of abortion, this pill produced most of the physical aftereffects of abortion, and my friend was sick in bed all day with stomach cramps. When she got pregnant again later, she decided to have an abortion. She told me that the abortion was actually less painful than the pill.

Another sorority member learned she was pregnant while dating a fraternity member in college. She agonized for six weeks before deciding to have an abortion, a decision she now regrets.

"I am always so nervous about getting pregnant now," she confided. "I'm always on the pill, and whenever I have sex, I always make sure whoever I'm with is wearing a condom.

"I hate seeing little kids because I think about how old my twin babies would be, and I wonder how my life would be different if I had kept them . . . or if they were boys or girls or one of each . . . or if I really killed them . . . I would never be able to have another abortion."

The only woman I knew who kept her baby instead of having an abortion was an acquaintance from a rival sorority. The baby's father was from the fraternity where I was a Little Sister. The guy didn't want to give up his fraternity life and face the responsibility of fatherhood, so his girlfriend dropped out of her sorority, moved home, had her baby, and finished college—all without his support. To this day, the child has never seen his father.

An unplanned pregnancy is a terrifying and confusing predicament. In the midst of the already intense pressures of college, it's the last thing students need to face. But it happens all the time.

GENITAL WARTS AND PUBIC LICE

Another problem in the Greek system is the prevalence of genital warts and pubic lice, or "crabs." They were so common, in fact, that I heard many students joke about them. Just about everyone I knew had contracted one or the other, at least once. Fraternity members usually roomed together with three or four others, sleeping on bunk beds, sharing towels, and often adopting a less-than-sanitary lifestyle. When one of them contracted a disease, another or all of his roommates caught it as well.

• Genital warts, or the human papilloma virus, are similar to warts found elsewhere on the body. Sometimes, however, a growth may resemble a wart but is actually an early symptom of either cancer or syphilis. In fact, certain types of genital warts are also associated with cancer.[6]

• "Crabs" are blood-sucking lice which usually appear only in the pubic hair around the anus. The louse, which can be clearly seen if you look closely, is one to two millimeters across, and resembles a tiny, flat crab.[7]

I was surprised that I made it through college without ever getting crabs. These scratchy, tiny pests are extremely annoying, and can last a few weeks, even with treatment.

"I got crabs a few times and I would agonize over it," confided one fraternity member. "It was just so gross, having insects crawling all around your private parts. They always made me want to scratch in places where it would offend others, so I was always running to the bathroom to have a good scratch. They made open wounds on my skin that left blood marks in my underwear."

Often these crabs weren't completely killed off, he said, because they would just go from person to person.

Getting genital warts is no laughing matter either, as I can personally attest. I always dreaded seeing my gynecologist, but I had to go to get birth-control pills. During one visit, while lying on the examining table in the usual humiliating position, I was told that a genital wart on my cervix would have to be removed.

"This shouldn't hurt too much," the doctor said. "I'm going to melt it off."

First he dilated my cervix with an instrument called a speculum, then inserted another instrument, doing something that felt as if my insides were being scratched. When he was finished, he gave me a sanitary pad to catch the bloody discharge. But the worst part was the painful cramps that lasted the rest of the day.

Unfortunately, that wasn't the last time I had to endure the uncomfortable process. When the wart returned, I had to endure the procedure two more times before it was gone. The only reason I didn't skip the treatment altogether was because the doctor warned me that without it I would be at risk of getting cancer.

AIDS

Obviously, the most lethal result of careless and risky sex is contracting AIDS. Acquired immune deficiency syndrome (AIDS) is caused by the human immunodeficiency virus (HIV). HIV is transmitted from one person to another by sexual intercourse, including oral sex; by using needles contaminated with an HIV carrier's blood; by the transfusion of contaminated blood products; in only a handful of cases, by body fluids of an HIV carrier; and sometimes from an infected pregnant woman to her fetus.

According to a Center of Disease Control Surveillance Report, throughout December 1995, there have been 319,849 reported deaths by AIDS. There are 513,486 persons with AIDS in the United States and 18,955 of those reported are from age twenty to twenty-four. In a 1990 survey of seventeen thousand blood samples taken at nineteen universities throughout the U.S.A., twenty-five out of every five thousand men tested were HIV-positive, and one of every five thousand women tested were HIV-positive.[8] These rates would probably increase significantly if students who indulge in alcohol, drugs, and risky sexual behavior—which many Greek members do—were targeted.

The reported number of people with HIV and AIDS is likely to go up. People may put off getting tested unless symptoms begin to appear. An average of eight years passes before a HIV infection overwhelms the body's defenses and worsens into AIDS, which is fatal.

"I think eventually, we will know a lot of people who find out that their behavior during college cost them their lives. Right now, I am only speculating who those people are," a recent sorority member and graduate explained.

A recent fraternity member and graduate, who has worked on AIDS research, explained, "Even if someone we know has found out that they have it, I think they would wait as long as they could before telling anyone. They would not want to be criticized for their past behavior. Many people . . . would not be supportive."

AIDS is irreversible. No cure yet exists; most people with HIV develop AIDS, deteriorate, and die. To avoid the ultimate regret, we must protect ourselves, always.

OTHER SEXUALLY TRANSMITTED DISEASES

Besides AIDS, there are many other harmful diseases that can be transmitted sexually—diseases to which Greek students are particularly vulnerable, given their casual attitude about sex. Each year, eight million people under the age of twenty-five catch a sexually transmitted disease other than AIDS. The infection rates are highest among Americans age fifteen to twenty-five, and the rates show few signs of declining.[9] Some of these diseases include syphilis, gonorrhea, chlamydia, and herpes.

• Syphilis produces an often painful sore on the genitals or mouth. The sore will slowly disappear even without treatment, but that doesn't mean the disease has gone away. Several weeks later, other signs will appear, including fever, sore throat, sores, or rashes.

• Gonorrhea can cause women to experience a burning sensation during urination, vaginal discharge, fever, or stomach pain—or, it may produce no signs or symptoms at all. A man will notice a whitish discharge from his penis, and will feel itching or burning during urination. Symptoms usually appear between one and five weeks after contracting the disease. Currently, 15 percent of gonorrhea strands are resistant to penicillin, tetracycline, or a combination of both.[10]

• Chlamydia, which often produces no symptoms in women, is the most prevalent sexually transmitted disease in the country. It's responsible for several other diseases that, if left untreated, cause sterility or blindness.

One sorority senior confided that she has been permanently affected since contracting chlamydia during her freshman year. The fraternity pledge with whom she was having sex had chlamydia, and didn't even know he had it.

"He had just transferred from another college, and I actually waited a month before I had sex with him, which was unheard of in college," she said. "I guess he had it before he came to our school."

At her annual checkup during her sophomore year, she learned that she had had chlamydia for almost a year. "Now the doctors say there is a good possibility that I will never be able to have children," she said. "I won't know for sure until I try. I was devastated, because I love children."

She said that even after several years, she still hates her former boyfriend so much that she can't stand to be in the same room with him. "If I run into him at a party or something, I still have to leave immediately."

• Herpes (HSV-2) can produce symptoms either extremely

painful or very mild. A man will notice a small sore or cluster of blisters on his penis. A woman may have fever and headaches, and will develop blisters in or around her vagina. Symptoms may disappear within a week or two without treatment, but the herpes virus never leaves the body. Herpes is incurable.[11]

A sorority alumnus who graduated three years ago said that she contracted herpes from a guy with whom she went home occasionally after a fraternity party or a night at the local college bar.

"We basically just used each other for sex," she said. "We did not want to be committed to each other; we just wanted to have a good time. I knew he was probably having sex with another girl; I just never asked him because I didn't want to know."

She said living with herpes has changed her life tremendously. She finds it difficult to be intimate with anyone because she hates having to tell them she has the disease. "It sounds so awful," she said. "I'm just afraid guys think of me as a slut after I tell them."

She added that she has been very careful since she got herpes, but that the guys she dates never want to stay in the relationship when they learn they would have to wear condoms the rest of their lives and be repeatedly checked for the disease.

"People just don't realize the endless hassles it creates," she said, adding that she now regrets being so promiscuous in college. "Most of my friends slept with guys they hardly knew at the end of the night, so I didn't think there was anything wrong with what I was doing."

When people contract any of these diseases, serious consequences can result if they aren't treated by a physician immediately. Some of the dangers include irreparable damage to female reproductive organs, sterility in men and women, arthritis, heart disease, or eye infections serious enough to result in blindness. Some of these symptoms show up years after a disease is first contracted, so those infected may not even know they are passing it on to their sexual partners.[12]

THE SPREAD

Although most sexually transmitted diseases can be treated, many students are too embarrassed, fearful, or irresponsible to go in for treatment. Going to see a gynecologist or a urologist is uncomfortable, to say the least, but many Greek students I knew thought it horrifying, especially if they believed they may have contracted a sexually transmitted disease.

Actually, even those who didn't think anything was wrong avoided getting checkups; they considered exposing themselves in front of a doctor too unpleasant. "I hate to see the gynecologist," one sorority member admitted. "Even when I had really bad infections or diseases, I waited for weeks, hoping they would go away."

Although such attitudes are understandable—many other women feel the same way—they also increase the risk of more extensive damage from a disease that goes undiscovered and untreated.

Besides not getting treatment, I also found that even when Greek members knew they had a sexually transmitted disease, they often didn't tell their sexual partners. It's fairly common to hear about a sorority member hating a fraternity member for giving her a disease, or vice versa. One fraternity member didn't tell his girlfriend that he had herpes because he feared she wouldn't go out with him anymore if she knew. Instead, he hoped she would never get it, or that she would never find out he had it—as if ignoring it would make the disease disappear.

When the woman eventually contracted herpes from him—which is almost always the result when unprotected sex continues—she was devastated. And when she found out that she would need treatment for the rest of her life, his fear was realized; she never wanted to see him again.

"I guess she was mostly mad because I didn't tell her I had the disease, but I never thought she would break up with me if she got it," the member said.

In spite of the risk of AIDS and other sexually transmitted

diseases, researchers have found that among college students the fear of AIDS has little or no bearing on whether or not they practice protected sex. They have also found, however, that those who fear AIDS are more likely to be monogamous.[13]

Studies have also found that fraternity members are less likely than other college students to practice safe sex. In a 1990 study, researchers found that although fraternity and sorority members have a clear understanding of AIDS, they rarely take the necessary safety precautions. In fact, fraternity members were reported to be the least cautious among college students.[14] While I was in college, many Greeks practiced unsafe sex so often that they thought they probably had already contracted AIDS. Many of the fraternity members were convinced they had it, so they felt there was no reason to confirm their fears by being tested. Sorority members, too, frequently reported having unprotected sex; they preferred to ignore the risk.

A friend of mine was certain he had AIDS, and finally, after great persuasion, agreed to go in and be tested. I was nervous for him, but he actually felt somewhat relieved just by having been tested. A few days later, he learned that he was not infected. From that day on, he vowed, he would protect himself and others by practicing safe sex.

Many more, however, continue their reckless sexual lifestyle, almost indifferent to the possibility they will contract the disease or infect others. "I try not to think about it," explained a fraternity member who refused to get tested for the HIV virus. "I probably do have it, but I would rather die than find out. I mean, your life is over once you know you have it—you know you're going to die, so what would be the point of living?"

"I hate even to watch TV or movies about it," another fraternity member confessed. "I look at them as they get really skinny, with spots all over their faces, and I think, 'That might be me soon.' It scares the hell out of me."

Another fraternity member told me he was afraid of getting AIDS, but that he still wouldn't change his sexual practices or start wearing condoms. "I know I'm at a high risk just from sleeping around with all these sluts who make it so easy for me not to wear a condom," he said. "I mean, I know they say guys are supposed to be just as responsible as women, but if a chick isn't going to make me wear one, I'm sure as hell not going to say anything."

All too often, fraternity members—like many grown men—refuse to wear condoms, complaining that they are uncomfortable and inconvenient. Many say that stopping to put on a condom "ruins the moment," or spoils the sensation and feeling of sex. Others argue the birth-control function by claiming they are sterile. And finally, albeit amazingly, many men say their penises are too large to fit into a condom—a preposterous claim, since condoms have been shown to fit over medium-sized watermelons without breaking.

These arguments and excuses echo the results of a 1991 study of fraternity men. Researchers found that less-frequent condom use in fraternities was attributed to the beliefs that condoms are uncomfortable, inconvenient, and disruptive to the mood, and limit physical sensation.[15]

The same study examined the frequency of condom use, monogamous relationships, and having multiple sexual partners among fraternity men. Within the monogamous subgroup, 32 percent reported that they always used a condom, as compared to only 10 percent in the subgroup that engaged in sex with multiple partners. My primary purpose for citing this study is to highlight the infrequent use of condoms, since we already know that many fraternity men frown on monogamous relationships.

Though less frequently used, another reason fraternity members cite for not wearing a condom during sex is that often they are simply too drunk to put a condom on. "After a long night of partying, the last thing anyone wants to do is to try to find a condom and put it on," said one fraternity member who refuses to wear them. Even if a man finds the patience and coordination to put on a condom in such a drunken state, he will likely put it on improperly, which will cause it to tear or break, and thus provide no protection anyway.

If it seems as though the finger is being pointed at fraternity men, it isn't. Women are equal partners in the failure to practice safe sex. One sorority member explained that she no longer insists her partners wear a condom because of previous failed attempts. "Twice it rolled off inside me," she explained. "Sometimes I still request that a guy wear one. But it hasn't worked out so many times that I never press the issue."

She added that using a condom seemed too difficult when either she or her partner was drunk or on drugs. "I guess you just get lazy because you are having such a great time, and dealing with putting on a condom is a buzz kill," she concluded.

I didn't force the issue, either. I heard all the excuses so often that I believed them; I actually thought it would be cruel to make my partner wear a condom.

In the end, of course, no matter how "uncomfortable" or "inconvenient" wearing a condom might be, nothing is more uncomfortable or inconvenient than dying from AIDS. As maturing young adults, it is important to be aware that the threat of AIDS and other sexually transmitted diseases does exist, and that people must behave responsibly to prevent its spread. Before you engage in unprotected sex, ask yourself this question: "Is one night worth my health, or my life?"

Clearly, the answer is "no." If you are incapable of abstaining, at least be prepared to protect yourself with a male or female condom—a sober mind wouldn't hurt, either. If you think you may have contracted AIDS, get tested immediately, for you are jeopardizing not only your own life, but the lives of others as well. And if you are considering having unprotected sex with someone, make sure he or she has been tested and that you trust him or her to tell you the truth.

A CONTINUOUS BATTLE

The concern for young adults who do not practice safe sex grows stronger every day.

Today, messages of prevention flood the airwaves. Unfortunately, so do images of sexual prowess and promiscuity.

While the Greek environment is definitely a contributor to risky sexual behavior in college students today, it is not the sole culprit. Today's college students are from the MTV generation—a generation that after ten years of television viewing has seen more than 92,000 scenes of sexual activity.[16] They are a generation that idolizes sex.

But for many, being sexually "hip" creates too much responsibility, especially for those who have been drinking or are on drugs. They are so consumed with fitting into this overwhelming, sexually-charged social structure that they don't think about their future. They purposely don't think about pregnancy, or the potential of contracting AIDS or other sexually transmitted diseases, until it's too late. Only then do they learn that invincible attitudes and carefree sex can cause serious psychological and physical effects over the long term.

It may be, too, that young people today resent the fact that they are the generation who has to think about the future every time they have sex—that is, if they want to have a future.

While today's young people have such an arduous burden to carry, they are also equipped with a better understanding of ways to protect themselves. Between public service announcements on television and in print, and campus literature and guest speakers provided by many universities today, college students are being warned. And Greek students may receive even more educational programming than non-Greeks.

Fraternities usually offer speakers at fraternity and interfraternity events, which focus on everything from abstinence and safe sex to the results of sexual activity and AIDS. The Fraternities' Commission on Values and Ethics has also created case studies that put students in fictional, yet probable, circumstances where they are forced to make decisions regarding their sexual activities. These case studies are available from the National Interfraternity Conference. The address may be found in the resources section at the back of this book.

There are other helpful and preventative measures both students and administrators can take, as well. For example, they can prohibit overnight guests on the nights when there are parties, place condom dispensers offering both male and female condoms in fraternity and sorority bathrooms, and recruit students who have been diagnosed with HIV or who are dying of AIDS to share their experience and relay the reality of practicing unprotected sex.

And finally, any changes made to help lessen the use of drugs or alcohol among Greek members (which was discussed in the previous chapter) would also help students use better judgment when making decisions regarding sex. "You are aware how alcohol can effect sexual activity," said a member of the National Interfraternity Council, "so fraternity members are at more risk."

6
RUSH AND PLEDGING

Exhausted and trying to relax in front of the rush counselor's office, I couldn't wait for it all to be over. It was the fourth day of rush, and the other rushees and I were about to find out which sororities had invited us back for the final round of parties. The sororities had stayed up late the night before making their selections, cutting more than half of the rushees from the list. I knew I would be crushed if I wasn't invited back to my top three sorority choices.

While we waited, I thought back over the flurry of parties of the last three days. Names and faces were now a blur, since most of the parties had gone like the first one.

It was a hot summer day when the other rushees and I were led into a large, crowded room decorated in floral pastels. Everyone talked so loudly that I could hardly hear as they offered me lemonade. I was hot and thirsty, but too nervous to accept it.

After the rushees were led to some chairs to sit down, two or three sorority women knelt on the floor around me. They pummeled me with enthusiastic questions: "What's your major?" "Where are you from?" "Do you have a boyfriend?" Each one acted as if my answers were the most fascinating they had ever heard.

I tried to smile and show my teeth as I answered that yes, I did have a boyfriend, and I was a communications major from nearby Tustin in Orange County.

"I know lots of people from Tustin!" a pretty blonde named Kelly chimed in. "That's great! Your parents must be so glad you're close enough to go home on the weekends. What do they do for a living, and where do they work?"

I was prepared for this question, though I knew my answer would mark off some points. "My parents are divorced," I explained. "My father owns a cellular phone company in Tustin, and my mother works for a designer clothing store in San Francisco."

Kelly shot a peculiar look at the women on either side of her. "Oh, I see. Do you ever see your mother? San Francisco is such a great city!"

I suddenly realized how warm the room was, and I felt dizzy and claustrophobic as I continued answering their questions. I could only wonder what repercussions my answer would create.

Soon a sorority sister rang a bell, announcing that the party was over. Each one said goodbye to me by name, reading it off my name tag, and began singing a fast song about their sorority as we walked out. Already we were being motioned on to the next house.

Once outside, I was relieved. That party was already a blur in my mind as I hurried on to the next one. Throughout the week I tried to ignore a nagging thought: These parties were so short and shallow, how could anyone tell if I belonged in their group? They weren't getting to know the real me—and I certainly wasn't getting to know them.

All I could do was make the best first impression possible—as they were doing. But what if we made a mistake?

Now, standing in front of the counselor's office, I was thankful it was almost finished. Most of the parties were over, and it was time to learn the decision.

Suddenly the rush counselor emerged from her office and called the first name on the list. A slender brunette with a small, upturned nose jumped up and disappeared into the office. Moments later, she emerged with her head held high, a look of arrogance across her face. She gave us a quick smirk as she left the building. We all knew she had what it took to be one of the select few. I longed to be like her.

Next, a petite woman with short, mousy blonde hair and a warm smile was called into the office. The rest of us sat tensely as the moments ticked away. Ten minutes later, she came running out, her hands partially covering her red, puffy eyes. She quickly escaped out the door without a backward glance. Would that be me?

"Esther Wright," the counselor called. My body went numb, but I forced myself to walk toward the room that held my future fate. As I sat down stiffly in the counselor's office, it felt as if the room were spinning. She handed me the schedule. With difficulty, I scanned it. Two of my selected houses were not on the list! My heart sank. What had I done to make them reject me?

The counselor tried to encourage me, explaining that I had lots of other houses to choose from. She didn't seem to understand that I only considered one worthwhile. All I could do now was keep trying for that one. I swallowed my self-pity and tried to compose myself before I left, realizing I was honored to be invited back at all.

I went on to be accepted into the sorority of my choice—but not everyone I knew was so lucky. One of my friends thought she was breezing through rush, but ended up with no house at all. Although she later rushed again and pledged a less-popular sorority, her animosity toward me began to grow. Our relationship has never been the same—all because of the elite system of rush.

In essence the sorority and fraternity rush process is a no-win situation, cultivating elitism at its worst. Those who aren't accepted may be devastated, like the woman who ran out of the counselor's office in tears. She and others rejected by the organizations of their choice may be deeply wounded by what they believe is a well-deserved commentary on their self-worth.

Upon closer scrutiny of the system, however, should we really believe that we are somehow worth less than others simply because we are rejected from what is considered an elite social group? Time and distance may show us not to base self-esteem on what others think of us—but when it happens, rejection by a sorority or fraternity can be seen as the end of the world.

And what of those who are accepted by the organization of their choice? Surely rush is a winning situation for them, many would say.

While acceptance into the Greek system may be a cause for rejoicing, rush is a no-win situation even for those asked to pledge. For with the coveted bid and affirmation of self-worth comes a reason to—and the expectation that one should—feel superior. Greek organizations ostracize members who associate with someone from a so-called lesser sorority or fraternity, or worse, with a non-Greek. Just like the woman who left the rush counselor's office with her nose in the air, the accepted few often come to believe they are better than everyone else because they were selected into an elite society.

What they forget is that they were accepted into the group for largely superficial reasons: appearance, family status and wealth, manners, and a positive first impression. They overlook the rush system itself. With its short week of parties, little time is available to evaluate someone on anything other than trivial, shallow factors. So, for the most part, pledges are selected by how they appear on the surface.

Actually, if we look closely at those who participate in rush, we'll find there's not much difference between those who are accepted and those who are not. According to a recent study, a much greater difference lies between students who choose not to take part in rush and those who do—whether they are invited to pledge or not. Researchers found that "those who chose to rush a sorority were more physically attractive, came from a wealthier family background, used alcohol more frequently, were higher in need of exhibitionism, and were more willing to attend parties where they might not fit in than students who did not rush a sorority."[1]

THE DEVELOPMENT OF RUSH

Initially, entry into sororities and fraternities was restricted to college seniors. The Greek system began to allow membership of all classes by the end of the nineteenth century. Gradually, the large increase in the number of people attempting to join the Greek system prompted sororities and fraternities to develop the more exclusive rush system in place today.

Fraternities still use the original rush method, where individuals are selected throughout a specified rush week. Selection is reserved exclusively for fraternity members; rushees are not allowed to select which fraternities they prefer. Often, rushees aren't invited to pledge by any group.

Sororities adopted "preferential bidding" about sixty years ago, a system originally developed by the medical field to match students with jobs. Preferential bidding allows sororities to rank their preferred rushees, while rushees rank their preferred sororities. Rushees, however, are only accepted into the sorority of their choice if the sorority also chooses them. And often these matches do not correspond.[2]

The College Panhellenic Council (CPC)—the group that decides the rules of rush—published a rush instruction manual, but neither it nor the workshops offered by the CPC give any advice as to what should be done for rushees who do not make it into the sorority of their choice, or into any sorority at all.

In fact, according to the manual, "Panhellenic strongly urges each sorority to re-invite . . . only those rushees they are seriously considering for membership. This will enable both the rushees and the sororities to know 'how they stand' early in the formal rush period."[3]

Such an attitude fosters elitism, and ignores those values upon which the Greek system was originally founded, "to promote the ideals of community, of brother and sisterhood, and to support educational and spiritual objectives."[4] In a study that analyzed reasons for deciding to rush a sorority, the deciding factors that sororities use to select members, and how rush rejection affected college women, researchers reported that its major flaw is that so many rushees are not invited to pledge or don't get matched with the organization of their choice.[5]

We need to evaluate the original purpose of the Greek system. Is it an inclusive network to provide students with a healthy social outlet, or a discriminatory vehicle to weed out undesirables?

COMPETITION

For the two weekends, five-, three-, or seven-day collection of parties known as rush, college students are put under intense scrutiny. Because fraternities and sororities must select a small pledge class from hundreds, sometimes thousands, of students in only one week, rush has become far more competitive and unpredictable than can be imagined.

The Greek system considers this process to be the most democratic procedure possible for recruiting new members, but, as we've stated, the factors used to select new pledges are prejudiced and predetermined. Rush can be a humiliating and insulting experience, even for rushees who are invited to pledge the organization of their choice.

The College Panhellenic Conference recommends that rush is held only once a year, early in the fall, "as close as possible to the start of the academic year, and conducted in as short a period of time as possible."[6] While a short rush period may have benefits—lessening the duration of such extreme pressure for rushees, for one—it forces sororities to make serious character judgments in a very short time. But this time limit alone causes members to focus on irrelevant factors and superficial criteria to determine someone's potential value to the organization.

APPEARANCE

From research and my own experience, I've found that the primary factor for judging students during rush is their appearance. Weight, height, style of dress, voice, hair style, and jewelry are all of utmost importance.

Social etiquette is another significant factor closely examined during rush. This includes how rushees hold themselves, how well they keep their smiles, and their ability to captivate peers. Wealth, or perceived wealth, also plays a serious role. Both sororities and fraternities consider freshmen more desirable, so their new pledges will pay membership dues and possibly live in the house for the longest time possible.

Any other determining factors are drawn from the rushees' registration sheets, short biographical sketches containing students' high school involvement, grade point averages, and the all-important information about their parents' affluence.

The chosen officer responsible for discovering skeletons in the closets of the rushees also researches each one's reputation. If any negative rumors come out, it's practically impossible to be accepted, especially into the more elite sororities and fraternities. And coming from the other side of the country doesn't exempt someone from these detailed investigations—sororities and fraternities have an amazing networking system to check up on everyone.

During the week of rush, sorority and fraternity members may secretly take notes on whom they like or dislike, then stay up late each night during rush, hashing and rehashing whom to invite back before taking a vote. One sorority rush chairman described a time when the entire sorority argued for three hours about one woman who was well-liked by some, but called names by others. "She was already at the bottom of our list because she had such bad grades," the rush chairman recounted. "Our advisor ended up making the final decision—and there was no way she was going to let that girl in. But another girl whose grades were just as bad got the bid because the advisor said she was from a good family."

A fraternity rush chairman reported what his brothers look for in a new pledge. "We want guys who are good looking, like to party, get lots of chicks, and will sell out for our house."

Their goal, he said, was to get twenty-five to thirty qualified pledges during rush each fall. At the rush parties, fraternity members first interview each rushee to get to know them and gather general information, sometimes taking notes of their impressions.

"If I could tell that a rushee did not have what it took to be in our house, I just wouldn't spend time talking to him," he explained.

At the end of the evening, he said, the brothers gathered to discuss the pros and cons of the rushees before voting on each one. Fewer than five negative votes meant a rushee would receive a bid to pledge the next night. It didn't bother the rush chairman that there was so little time to judge the candidates.

"If the guy ended up not having what it took to be in our house, we could just drop him later, or when he was pledging," he concluded.

STARS AND LEGACIES

As an active member in my sorority, I quickly learned that each rushee was to be led into a certain room according to an unspoken ranking system. The most important rushees for us to meet right away were the "stars" and the "legacies."

A "star" was a rushee possessing all of the most desirable qualities. All members were encouraged to go to the star room to get to know them and try to get them to like our group.

The "legacies"—those who had a parent, sibling, or grand-parent in the same sorority or fraternity—were not always accepted. Greeks are strongly encouraged to accept legacies out of loyalty to past members, but they can decide not to accept them as long as they make the decision by the third day of rush.

"All the girls were supposed to make an extra effort to talk to the star girls and really try to get them to like the house," a sorority member recalled. "We had to be sure to check out the legacies, to pick out anyone who was fat or ugly so we would be able to remember to vote them out as soon as possible."

Clearly, this is a system of elitism. Sorority members are taught to value people not on the basis of their abilities and personality, but on family background, reputation, and looks.

ATMOSPHERE

With the time constraints and superficial elements that dominate rush, it is no wonder students are forced toward an atmosphere of phoniness.

First, Greeks do all they can to influence rushees to select their organization, because they want to have the option of dropping a rushee rather than being dropped by a rushee first. Greeks believe it's crucial to have as many quality rushees as possible from whom to choose, especially the last night.

I've seen some fraternity and sorority members grow so desperate for good pledges that they make promises to individual rushees, or even try to confuse rushees by making a competing group look bad. Most college Greek councils have rules against fraternities and sororities demonstrating such unethical behavior during rush, but rushees are usually unaware of those rules.

During rush at most campuses, Greek organizations battle harshly against one another for the best pledges. Afterward, the new pledge classes are rated—and that "grade" will often predict the future reputation of the sorority or fraternity. A few days after I became a pledge, I found out that my pledge class, along with the thirteen other pledge classes, had been ranked, along with our pictures, in the school and Greek newspapers.

I later learned that if a "number one" house receives a mere "average" rating on their pledges, from then on that house is considered average—unless they can somehow reclaim their position the next year with a better pledge class.

These factors make rush into a trite, artificial situation for both Greeks and rushees. This same phony atmosphere was described by a fraternity member, who confided that they always drank alcohol during rush to enable them to be more relaxed and friendly.

"The rushees had no idea, because we would keep all the alcohol in one of the rooms they were not allowed in," he explained. "I would go around meeting the rushees for a half hour, go back to the room, have a few shots and drink a beer, then go back to the party." He said that many brothers used drugs in the same way. "We just had to try to hide it from the rushees, in case there were any dorks that might tell the Greek council," he said. "If the Greek council found out, they might not let us finish having rush for that semester."

He added that their fraternity didn't bribe rushees—because of the risk—but once they reported a rival fraternity who had bribed two rushees who were torn between the two houses. "We found out they had taken them two nights in a row to a strip bar in a limousine, buying them drinks and showing them a good time," he said. "They even offered to pay for any of the strippers to go home with them."

Artificiality is especially seen on Preference Night, the last part of sorority rush where sisters work especially hard to play up to the rushees. Dressed in semiformal attire, gathering for dinner or dessert, the sororities make the evening emotional and sentimental, emphasizing the close friendships they have with each other. The night is spent singing ballads, performing rituals, and giving the rushees personalized letters from sorority members stating their love for the rushee. It's all designed to make rushees feel as if they already belong, and that the sorority sisters are the closest friends they will ever have.

At both of the houses I visited on Preference Night, most of the women were crying and hugging each other the entire time. The first house dimmed the lights and performed a candle-passing ceremony. First they lit each other's candles one by one, then lit the rushees' candles, as if we were already part of the sorority.

At the other sorority party I attended, the members gave us pearl necklaces identical to ones they were wearing. When the party ended, they each took their necklace off and placed them into a large water-filled seashell. Then they did the same with our necklaces, symbolizing the close bonds we could form by joining their sorority.

While there is nothing wrong with these rituals and sentimentality, I found that all too often it was just for show. As an impressionable rushee, I was swept along by the glamour of being in this elite group, but I was to find later that the bonds weren't as close as they first appeared. The emotions displayed on this night were actually a thin veneer hiding the many problems outlined in this book.

DESPERATION

Many new students on campus are desperate to be accepted during rush. They believe that belonging to a good fraternity or sorority is the only way to make friends and have a social life in college. This belief causes some to become so frantic that to get in, they sacrifice their self-respect and subject themselves to humiliating practices.

This is especially true in Little Sister rush for the more popular fraternities. As a Little Sister myself for two years, I helped with four rush parties where I saw women obsessed with the idea of hanging out with the guys in our house. The Little Sister rush chairman told me some were so desperate to join that they would come right out and ask what they had to do to get in.

That's when they learned that they could earn an early bid before the voting took place by performing "personal favors" for brothers. These favors were always sexual: anything from oral sex to two rushees having sex with one brother. The rush chairman simply kept blank bid cards with him at each party, and as brothers requested a certain woman, he filled in the names and handed them out right there.

"Everyone was always extremely drunk at these parties," my friend recounted, "and most of the girls were more than willing to cooperate."

That night during the voting, any member who received a favor stood up and named the new Little Sister, describing in detail what sexual favor she performed, and often rating it. These activities were highly encouraged because it was a way for fraternity members to quickly learn who was "easy." The rush chairman told me that usually, at least a dozen women got early bids this way during two nights of rush.

REJECTION

As a Little Sister, I also had opportunity to help the fraternity rush new brothers, a privilege many fraternities don't give women. I will never forget seeing both the jubilation of those accepted and the devastation of those rejected, especially one night during my sophomore year.

It was the third night of rush. I arrived at the house early, with nine other Little Sisters, who were all wearing short dresses and high-heels—we were there mainly for decorative purposes. The fraternity members also looked their best, sporting dress slacks, loafers, ties, pressed shirts, and fraternity pins.

As soon as the rushees started arriving, I stood behind a table by the door, greeting them and asking them to sign in. The fraternity had already selected five guys to whom they planned to give bids that night, and secretly I recorded my own list of favorite guys. Our opinions about the rushees were well respected, and I knew that throughout the night I would be continually introduced to young men, then later asked by fraternity members if I thought they had "what it took."

Half an hour after the party started, the other Little Sisters and I were talking to several rushees when my boyfriend called me over to meet Jeff, one of the special five. I shook his hand, trying to charm him as we talked for a few moments. As soon as another brother came up to meet Jeff, my boyfriend made our excuses and drew me into another room.

"What do you think of Jeff?" he asked. He was well dressed, good-looking and confident. He seemed deserving to me.

"You should give him a bid," I said.

"Yes, I think we will tonight. Did you meet Bob Thomas? He has light brown, longish hair."

"Maybe, but I can't remember."

"That's the problem. He seems like a dork to me. I need you and Tammy to ask him to leave. Will you?"

I didn't like it, but I agreed. Once I found Tammy, we both walked around the party, scanning the name tags of the rushees.

Tammy spotted him first. Talking to a fraternity member, Bob looked slightly straggly, dressed in wrinkled dress slacks and a collared shirt, Converse tennis shoes, and a shaggy haircut.

"Hi, you must be Bob," I interrupted. "Can we have a word with you?"

"Sure, I'd love to," he said, smiling. Though average looking, Bob had a pleasant smile. I hated what we had to do as we led him outside. Stopping, we turned toward him.

"Bob, we have to advise you to go to some other houses and not spend any more time here," I said, watching his cheerful face grow flustered. I knew this wouldn't be easy.

"I don't understand," he said in a shaking voice. "Are you telling me to leave? Is that what the *guys* want?"

"I'm afraid so—But there are lots of other houses," I began, but I could tell he had his heart set on ours.

"Did they tell you why? I mean, I'll leave, but I just don't understand why they don't like me. It seemed like they really liked me. So many of the guys said that they were glad to see me tonight, and they told me I was becoming one of them." His eyes were starting to gloss over, and I knew he was about to cry.

"Please don't make this any harder," I said. "They just think you'd fit in better at a different house, okay? I'm sorry." There was nothing more to say, so Tammy and I headed back to the fraternity house, leaving him to deal with the rejection.

When I told Tammy how bad I felt for him, she just laughed. "Who cares? He's a dork." I returned to the party, trying to forget about Bob and the grief he was feeling—and I knew several more similar confrontations would take place that night.

Suddenly, someone rang a dinner bell. All the fraternity members ran toward Jeff, who was holding a bid, proud to be their new pledge.

The guys gathered around Jeff, leaning against one another in a tight circle as they started singing a song. Just as I thought their new pledge would be smothered to death, the fraternity members lifted him above their heads. When the song was over, they set him down and began shaking his hand in congratulations.

The excitement over, it was then back to the business of weeding out the undesirables and giving bids to the "best"—all based upon appearances and first impressions. I doubt there was as big a difference between Bob and Jeff as they thought.

This system of rush, with its inherent rejection, is simply too harsh for young adults to endure: many are left devastated just as they begin the challenging academic schedule of college. Many students are unable to get over the rejection of being dropped by a particular house, and at least 14.6 percent of them quit rush entirely when they don't get asked back.[7]

A recent study of sorority rush found that, "rejection from a social group like a sorority could have tremendous effects on the lives of young college students." This rejection is especially devastating because it happens during the most stressful time in a student's life. From their own observations, researchers reported that sororities, through rush, were alienating others.[8]

Researchers from another study on the effects of sorority and fraternity rush on students' self-image reported, "the sense of disappointment that can accompany an unsuccessful rush experience can be particularly great if it occurs at the beginning of the freshman year, before the student has had an opportunity to make friends or build relationships. In some situations, it could even trigger a decision to leave college."

They added, "Because success or lack of success in rush can be perceived as a form of peer evaluation, failure to be accepted into a Greek-letter organization, or even one's preferred sorority or fraternity, can communicate a harsh message to students concerning their personal traits or ability to fit into the group."[9]

INSECURITY

Another type of elitism occurs once pledges are accepted. They are put on display, paraded around to promote the Greek organization they are pledging. Treating the pledges like a commodity, fraternities and sororities show off pledges, hoping their new recruits will get their house invited to all of the parties.

It's well known that fraternities and sororities are searching for new members who fit a particular mold. Those who don't conform will be rejected during rush or may be dropped at any time from the group—even after pledging or initiation. This impending rejection puts members in a position of insecurity that never leaves.

Many pledges live in fear that after three months of spending all their free time building friendships with their pledge class, they could be "de-pledged" or forbidden participation in the final initiation ceremony. Too often, pledges are devastated to find they will not be allowed to go to any events with their new friends who have all been initiated.

In a sorority, the most common reason pledges are asked to leave is because they do not achieve the expected grade-point average. My sorority required a 2.7 average by the end of the semester, which was difficult for many pledges. Most sorority pledges are freshmen facing a difficult transition into college classes, and find that the required activities of the sorority produce an added strain.[10]

In my own pledge class of about twenty women, four weren't allowed to become members with the rest of us. They were put on probation for a semester, forbidden to attend any sorority functions, yet still required to pay monthly fees. If they didn't achieve the required grades by the end of the next semester, they were usually voted out of the sorority.

Two close friends from my pledge class were voted to be dropped as pledges. "Getting voted out of my sorority by the girls I called my sisters and friends was one of the most devastating experiences I have ever been put through," one of them told me. She later dropped out of school.

I remember at the time feeling pressured to vote against my friends. Our national advisor came in before we voted, making threats about what would happen if we voted them in as members.

"Ladies, I cannot stress just how important it is for you to let this girl go. She obviously has some kind of incurable problem affecting her study habits. She is bringing down the entire house's grade-point average, and you know this will affect us during rush next fall.

"I know these girls are your sisters and friends, but if they are still in our sorority next semester, national will probably not allow you to have all five of your exchange parties. You really have no other choice."

It always amazed me that our house would vote to have our sisters leave, many of them forced to move out of the house, just because we might have one less party the next semester. Our loyalty was obviously to partying, not to one another.

Grades were not the only way a pledge was voted out, however. Some women got into trouble for improper social behavior, such as making a scene while drunk or for being sexually promiscuous. If a pledge got caught misbehaving, she was usually warned of her unacceptable conduct and put on probation. If the same pledge got in trouble again, the sorority council would meet to vote. Our sorority had a low tolerance for misbehaving pledges and members, usually voting to kick them out.

Fraternity pledges can be kicked out just because one of the members feels like it. A member explained to me that pledging for a fraternity is far from being guaranteed acceptance as a member. There were always a few pledges the members did not like who would get harassed and then voted out. If 70 percent or more did not like the pledge, for whatever reason, the pledge was given a vague explanation and told to leave.

In an average fraternity or sorority pledge class of twenty members, usually only thirteen will make it through the pledgeship. The others will either be dropped or quit on their own.

DISCRIMINATION

Shortly after I became a pledge, I got to know a woman in my biology class who was nice, smart, and funny. She was not in the Greek system—she was slightly overweight—but I thought she was great. After class we would go to the library or to her dorm for a popcorn snack, and sometimes met for lunch. We would spend hours laughing and talking about relationships, politics, philosophy, and psychology. She was one of the few people with whom I could hold an intelligent conversation.

One day, in the middle of that semester, we went to one of the more popular places on campus for a snack. Just as we walked into the food court, I saw a large group of my soon-to-be sorority sisters ahead of us. I knew they would not approve of my friend, and immediately felt uncomfortable.

I went up the group to introduce my friend, but even before

I said a word, my sisters were already looking at her disapprovingly. To my horror, the situation only got worse.

After I made the introductions, none of them said anything, and walked away haughtily. I was embarrassed, but even more felt ashamed to be a part of their group. I spent the rest of the day apologizing to my friend.

Later one of my sorority sisters cornered me. "Who was that fat girl you were with? What were you doing with her?"

I tried to explain she was a friend from my biology class, but she cut me off.

"You are not going to get initiated if you hang out with dorks like her," she warned. "You have plenty of new friends you should spend time with, not with some loser."

I didn't know what to say in response. After that, I tried to go places with my friend where Greeks were unlikely to go, but she quickly confronted me. She didn't want to be friends with someone who was ashamed of her.

I was torn. I really liked her, yet I thought I would be a fool to give up my new friends—seventy popular sorority sisters—for just one. After that, I never befriended anyone on campus who was not in my sorority.

Looking back, I regret my actions. I thought it was glamorous to be a member of an elite group, but it actually meant excluding many students with more important qualities.

THE QUESTION OF MUTUAL SELECTION

Most members of the National Interfraternity Council agree that it is unfortunate if the process of rush affects a student's self-esteem. However, there is both elation and disappointment on campus. Throughout the recruitment process, fraternities are encouraged to give rushees sufficient feedback. That way, if a rushee starts to get the feeling that rejection is inevitable, he will still have time to join another group. If a rushee does not get asked to join the house he wanted, the council would encourage the rushee to join another fraternity.

Members of the National Panhellenic Conference, on the other hand, do not feel that they should be concerned about hurting rushees' self-esteem. They consider rush a process of mutual selection, and a process that all sororities should continue in order to gain new members. One representative compared rush to the selection process for a theater production, or to attend a particular college. "Sorority membership is not for everyone," she added. "Through the rush process, that becomes more apparent than if you first go into it to see what it is."

National Greek representatives argue that after rush there are usually some houses a rushee can still join. Also, if students come out of rush without an invitation to pledge a house, they automatically go into the resource pool for continuous open bids. That way, if a house did not get the total number of pledges they were allowed, members can go to the open pool for bids.

THE WAY OF CHANGE

Many sororities are changing their format from the traditional five-day rush period. Rush can now be held prior to the fall semester or deferred into the second semester. A few campuses on the East Coast, including Yale University in New Haven, Connecticut, Dartmouth College in Hanover, New Hampshire, and the University of Hartford, West Hartford, Connecticut, are moving to sophomore rush. More emphasis is being placed on a continuous open bid system, so some sororities are rushing throughout the year. Most of these sororities still have a formal rush period, however, which can last for five days, three days, seven days, or two consecutive weekends with no rush during the weekdays.

For the most part, sororities have instituted these changes because the resource pool of freshman rushees is smaller than in past years. Fewer students are going through rush, and those who do are juniors and seniors who have transferred from another college, according to a National Panhellenic Conference member, adding that overall, university enrollment may not change—it even may grow—but those numbers reflect incoming juniors and seniors, rather than freshmen and sophomores.

These changes in rush periods are also the result of universities' refusal to provide housing for rushees before school begins. Because many sorority groups cannot afford hotels, they are moving rush to the start of school, when rushees have already been assigned housing.

Several fraternities are also making positive changes in the process of rush. The National Interfraternity Conference now encourages fraternities to invite other students to become members throughout the year, claiming that a year-round, open recruitment process seems to make more sense. After all, a fraternity member might befriend someone and want to ask him to join after rush has taken place.

At this time, fraternities hold rush in a variety of ways. Some have rush once or twice a year; others have a revolving door, where fraternity members can join at any time. In a revolving-door system, new pledges automatically start their pledge education or membership program when they join; it is on an individual basis. Fraternities can be more flexible in this regard because, unlike sororities, they have no quota to meet. One fraternity might bid two guys while another might bid two hundred.

But more needs to be done. At its most basic level, rush is a system of elitism. And while I don't pretend to have all the answers, there are some suggestions that warrant consideration.

First, instituting a longer, less formal rush would afford students the chance to get to know one another better before selecting a house to pledge or a rushee to bid. While this would not ease the pain of rejection for those not invited to bid, it would at least provide an opportunity to select students on the basis of character and personality, rather than appearance.

And though it may not always be possible to guarantee admittance into a particular house after preference night, students should at least be given the option of pledging one of their top three choices. Furthermore, once pledges become full-fledged members, a house should not be able to drop them, unless they have done something that is illegal or caused them to be expelled from school.

Of course, these are only some ideas for making rush a more positive experience for students who want to join the Greek system. What really needs to be addressed and corrected, however, is the underlying mindset of Greek students—and everyone—across the nation: the notion of image.

7

THE PERFECT GREEK IMAGE

Trying to hide my doubts, I looked at the smiling face of my sorority sister as she lay recovering in her hospital bed.

"They put a clear plastic tube in one side, then another in the other side, and vacuumed out the fat," Sherry recounted. "It was so weird, because I could see it coming out, but I couldn't feel anything.

"They couldn't take out more than a couple of soda bottles full, but it's better than nothing." She sighed and pointed to her thighs, which had been wrapped and were now covered by a tight pair of black spandex leggings.

As she continued describing her surgery of the day before, I couldn't help but wonder if it was all a mistake. I was happy she had gotten something she really wanted, but Sherry was already so glamorous and beautiful, did she really need the surgery?

Obsessed with the model-perfect image our house projected, Sherry was always dressed in the latest fashions and accessories, rarely wearing the same outfit twice. She regularly tanned and had her hair and nails done at the salon, assuring that she was always perfectly groomed. Yet in spite of her picture-perfect appearance, I knew she always felt uncomfortable and awkward in our sorority.

Each day before she went out the door, Sherry took time in front of the mirror, fastidiously applying makeup to her already gorgeous face. As beautiful as she was, it wasn't quite enough. Before she went out to face the critical and elitist attitudes of the Greeks, she would always turn to me or another sorority sister for reassurance.

"Do I look okay?" Sherry would ask, seemingly unaware that she could pass for a movie star. And no matter how many times she was reassured, she would ask again in just a few hours.

Standing in her hospital room, I knew that her surroundings had caused Sherry's exaggerated perception of the size of her hips. The sorority's obsession with beauty had gotten to her; she couldn't stand being not quite as skinny as most of the women.

Sitting on her bed, I listened to Sherry describe the procedure. She was thrilled with the results, believing thinner thighs would make her feel secure and happy. I felt bad for her. Never satisfied with herself, she had surgically altered part of her genetic makeup to better fit the sorority's ideal image. If that were the final answer, perhaps it would have been worth it—for her own peace of mind—but I knew that before long, she would find some other part of her body to change in her never ending quest to fit the Greek model of beauty. Nothing would change for Sherry until she realized that the answer didn't lie in her outer appearance, but in finding contentment within herself.

At the time, I was only beginning to learn this lesson myself. Like most of my sorority sisters, I was obsessed with striving for physical perfection. Something deep inside tried to remind me that we only find true peace within ourselves by learning to be content with our uniqueness, but so strong were the expectations of Greek society, which admired and respected women solely for their appearance, that I, too, was willing to go to any length to fit the perfect Greek image—even to the point of submitting to expensive plastic surgery myself. I would have had a number of surgeries, had I been able to find a way to pay for them.

Not until I was out of college and away from the Greek environment did I finally begin to see how little this thing called image mattered. Once I became a mother, it didn't seem so important anymore. Still, when I run into sorority friends from college, all too often they remain dissatisfied with how they look, though most of them are gorgeous and dressed in the latest fashions.

This perpetual quest for physical perfection affects not only Greek women, but men, too. Desiring the muscles of a professional bodybuilder, one of my closest friends in a fraternity became addicted to steroids.

Starting with pills, then shooting up with needles, Bill was elated to watch his muscles begin to swell. But the drug also resulted in his becoming easily irritated, aggressive, and violent. He constantly tried to pick fights with other guys, and was quickly losing friends. Even I took unwarranted verbal abuse every time he was around. Suspecting steroid use, I finally confronted him.

"What are you talking about?" he replied, incensed that I'd even suggest it. "How would I know anything about steroids? I've just been working out a lot!"

Soon after, Bill got into a violent fight with a longtime friend, giving Bill a real scare. He finally confessed to me that he was hooked on steroids, and that he'd been having bloody stools for some time. He was afraid that he might die if he continued his habit. Realizing he was out of control, he finally quit.

Not every Greek puts his or her own health and well-being at risk for perfect physical appearance, but stories like these are all too common. In this chapter, we'll examine how striving for the perfect physical image can lead Greek students to sacrifice their health, friendships, and even their own identity and contentment.

PRESERVING THE MOLD

Studies have shown that every fraternity and sorority holds a distinct image that members are expected to adopt. Some of these images include being sophisticated, conservative, jocks, wealthy, party-goers, drug-users, surfers or "beach babes," athletes, and so on.

Research on stereotypes shows that sorority and fraternity members are attracted to individuals that fit their image. In a specific study of students trying to join sororities, those who fit into the sorority's own stereotype received a higher rating of suitability to become members.[1] Evidently, the more a person fits a group's self-proclaimed image, the more that group will want him or her to join.

Once someone has joined a sorority or fraternity, he or she is expected to maintain the predetermined image of that particular house. In examining sororities during a study of idealized images, researchers found that compliance to group standards is maintained through subtle measures of social control.[2]

This was true in my own experience, and that of many sources as well.

A recent college graduate and sorority member said, "We were being molded a certain way, and pressured so much to fit in that most of us lost our own identity." She added that the expected image was reinforced through conversations sorority members had about their sisters. "Those who didn't conform stood out, and were usually thought of as weird . . . a member the computer had accidentally matched up with our sorority," she said.

It seems fraternities and sororities seek new members who fit their image because it makes it easier to mold and control their members into following the group. Selecting members who already fit the image of the house makes it much easier to convince them of the importance of maintaining that image.

The particular image of each fraternity or sorority is well known not only to its members, but also to students throughout the Greek system. Consequently, members are expected, and often pressured, to conform to that image not only by their organization, but also by the Greek system as a whole.

Even with the contrasting characteristics of each house, however, there is one, universal ideal throughout Greek society: physical beauty. Maintaining good-looking members makes a house popular, assuring that they will be asked to all the best parties, and boosting their rank in the Greek system.

As already discussed, most students who join the Greek system are at a vulnerable time in their lives, and have been found to be generally more insecure than other college students. For the first time, they are looking solely to peers for their self-worth and identity, rather than to their parents. The danger is that they are at greater risk of becoming obsessed with looking perfect, never being content with their appearance, and falling into harmful traps to achieve this ideal.

THE QUEST FOR MATCHLESS BEAUTY

The Greek system demands men and women to be beauty conscious, oftentimes excessively. In a study of sorority image, researchers found that these groups wholeheartedly embrace fashion and the beauty myth.[3]

Based on interviews and my own experience, I can personally attest to the fact that fraternities' values are no different. "In our fraternity," one member explained, "if a guy did not get the chicks or if he was ugly, he had better have a lot of money and drive a super-nice car. If not, he would get teased all the time."

In the *Greek Legend,* a yearbook for all the fraternities and sororities, the most popular section was always the "Gods and Goddesses" listing. This section featured only the most beautiful sorority members in bikinis, and the best-looking fraternity members displaying bare chests. The pressure to be beautiful was also evident when fraternities selected the prettiest sorority women to represent their main events or to serve as a showpiece during sale auctions. It is no wonder, then, that even the most attractive Greeks have the tendency to criticize their appearance.

For sorority members, the beautiful, physically fit, large-breasted stereotype is the ideal. A study found that women internalize this message, believing they should care a great deal about how they look, and at the same time internalizing a norm for thinness that is virtually unattainable for most.[4]

Fraternity members also play a strong role in reinforcing this ideal by being so vocal about wanting to be with a woman who fits the type so commonly featured on calendars, beer posters, and other advertising aimed at male audiences. Consequently, sorority members idolize super models, never satisfied with their own appearance.

One sorority member explained that being around fraternity guys in the Greek system caused her to constantly compare herself with the most beautiful women.

"For the first time, you are spending a lot of time with large groups of guys," she said. "So you hear their 'guy talk' and how obsessed they are with good-looking women."

Likewise, fraternity members are pressured to be attractive and muscular by the attitudes of sorority women.

"Girls always like the good-looking guys," a fraternity member explained. "The guys who go out with the best-looking girls are always the most popular."

The sorority women I knew in college were caught up with gaining status by going out with guys who were considered "babes." They always tended to flock around the best-looking fraternity men. And if a woman could snare him, that was the ultimate prize. Likewise, the fraternity member surrounded by the prettiest women was the one most respected by his fraternity brothers.

THE PERFECT GREEK IMAGE

PLASTIC SURGERY

So strong is the pressure to live up to such unrealistic standards of beauty that sorority and fraternity members will do anything to achieve the ideal, even plastic surgery. According to the Academy of Facial Surgeons, the number of cosmetic surgical procedures climbed 55 percent (from 322,035 to 501,000) between 1988 and 1993. In 1992, more than two-thirds of the procedures performed by the society's five thousand member surgeons were on patients aged nineteen to fifty.[5] From the number of my acquaintances who underwent surgery, I can attest that many of these patients are Greeks.

All too often, Greeks think they will gain instant popularity by the touch of a scalpel. Besides these expectations being unrealistic, there is also the potential risk that an operation will be unsuccessful and result in painful and possibly permanent scarring or other physical damage. And sometimes, patients end up disappointed with the lasting results of plastic surgery, occasionally preferring their appearance prior to the procedure. Of course, with plastic surgery—or any surgery, for that matter—there is always the chance that a patient may even die on the operating table.[6]

Clearly, choosing to have plastic surgery is an individual's right. What is so problematic with Greek students electing to have these procedures performed is their motivation. Young men and women are electing to change their bodies permanently based on a temporary feeling of pressure to fit in. I saw many Greek students make hasty decisions to submit to the knife, and regard it as lightly as if they were purchasing a new outfit and charging it on their credit card.

Retired plastic surgeon Dr. Thomas Rees, currently a professor of plastic surgery at New York University Medical Center and author of *More than Just a Pretty Face*, warns that the decision to have plastic surgery is unhealthy when the patient's reasons for doing so are tied to the expectations of others. "It's a very, very personal decision," he says.

Many mental-health professionals caution that patients can be set up for disappointment when they think surgery is the answer to all their problems. "These patients are expecting things you're never going to be able to deliver," Rees says.[7]

Plastic surgery was so common in my sorority that it was often discussed openly among members. Two members had so many surgeries done on their faces and bodies during one school break that we wouldn't have recognized them had they not told us who they were. One of them was even featured on the news, complete with before and after pictures, for being the youngest adult to have so many surgeries.

Another sorority member I know had her breasts greatly augmented in college. Now, in the corporate world, she regrets that she got such large implants.

"I was definitely influenced by the fraternities' 'big breasts are best' mentality," she said. "I was very insecure then, and impressionable. Getting the attention of these guys was very important to me. Now I feel like I cannot be taken seriously at work."

THE STEROID TRAP

Young men are also influenced by the strong emphasis on physical appearance, often becoming competitive about their body size, spending long hours working out. At times, this may lead fraternity members to use steroids, like my friend Bill. Of the fraternity men I knew, I have reason to believe that around 25 percent of them used steroids.

At one time, steroids were used only by athletes and hard-core bodybuilders, but doctors agree that today, fewer than 50 percent of steroid users are athletes.[8] Instead, this drug has become a way for fraternity men to obtain the body image they want in order to boost their popularity. Dr. Arthur Blouin, a psychologist at the Ottawa Civic Hospital in Ontario, Canada, says that young men "are willing to risk the side effects of steroids to avoid the negative perception that they are too small and weak."[9]

Dr. Howard P. Rome, editorial director of *Psychiatric Annals,* wrote in 1992 that narcissism was the underlying reason behind the intense competitiveness entwined in every aspect of twentieth-century society, and the key to the rise in the use of anabolic steroids among nonathletes with low self-esteem.[10]

Robert Katz, chief pharmacologist at Lancaster General Hospital, explained how the drug works. "Anabolic steroids bind with the male hormones in a cell," he said. "These cells then produce RNA (ribonucleic acid) and build more protein for more muscle growth and less fat production."[11]

Besides the personality changes many users experience, one harmful effect from steroid use is the possibility that the user's arteries will become clogged with cholesterol. Also, muscles may increase their strength more rapidly than the joints or tendons can handle, causing them to deteriorate or tear.

As humanmade derivatives of testosterone, anabolic-androgenic steroids (AAS) are not only dangerous, but costly. A five-week cycle of use costs $600 or more.[12] But the unknown price users pay may be even greater. Steroid use has been linked to serious illness and premature death. "The best-documented effects are those on the liver, serum lipids, and the reproductive system. . . . Use of AASs has been associated with self-reported changes in mood, behavior, and somatic perceptions. . . . Schizophrenia, increases in irritability, hostility, anger, aggression, depression, hypomania, psychotic episodes, and guilt have been reported among AAS users. Psychological dependence and withdrawal symptoms, including mood swings, violent behavior, rage, and depression, possibly severe enough to lead to thoughts of suicide, have also been reported after steroid cessation. In 1990, a study reported several cases of homicide and near-homicide by AAS users."[13]

EATING DISORDERS

In the quest for physical perfection, many sorority members become obsessed with losing weight. A recent Gallup Poll reported that 8 percent of women disliked or were totally repulsed by some part of their bodies, while 62 percent wanted to lose between eleven and twenty pounds. In a society where "thin is in," now more than ever, it's easy to understand why large social groups of women consider the lean look a crucial part of their body image.

Because of these pressures, many sorority members skip meals, exercise excessively, and take diet pills. Some develop full-fledged eating disorders such as bulimia or anorexia nervosa. In response to an article on the subject printed in our sorority magazine, one member wrote to the editor that she had suffered from an eating disorder for a number of years.

"My college days were particularly difficult," she wrote. "Not only are young collegiate women under pressure to succeed academically, they are under additional pressure to conform and be accepted socially."[14]

Evidence suggests that bulimia is quite prevalent among college women; estimates say 4 to 15 percent have serious problems with bulimia.[15] Bulimia is characterized by alternating periods of uncontrolled binge eating and periods of fasting, strict dieting, or "purging" the food through vomiting, diuretics, or laxatives.

In a study of self-induced vomiting among college women, it was found that 80 percent of high-frequency purgers were sorority members.[16] Researchers suggest that group membership, especially in groups composed of women of the same age, is at the heart of the transmission of bulimia, as members share their "secret new way to eat what they want without gaining weight."[17] Unfortunately, members do not share the secrets about health risks bulimics face, including fatigue, sore throats, ulcerated esophagi, tooth decay, heart disturbances caused by severe potassium depletion, and sometimes even death.[18]

One sorority member confided, "I hated going to dinner [at the sorority house], because all of these super-skinny girls would be sitting around the table, just getting back from working out, picking at their dinner and complaining that they were depressed because they were so fat."

She went on to say that sorority members seem to be especially body conscious because of the large number of Greek events that call for swimsuits, volleyball shorts, sexy formal dresses, or other revealing apparel.

"My roommate was bulimic, and it was so disgusting," she continued. "Our toilet was always clogging up and overflowing with barf, and she would always be in the bathroom after we went out drinking or eating."

According to medical surveys, anorexia nervosa affects 1 percent of female college students.[19] Characterized by the refusal to eat, anorexia nervosa leads to extreme loss of weight, hormonal disturbances, and eventually death. One woman who lived down the hall in my sorority house had a severe case of the disease. While everyone was downstairs eating their meals, Katrina was never there. Refusing to eat, she became more and more thin and gaunt.

By Christmas break, Katrina had to be hospitalized, and was forced to gain a little weight. She soon rejoined us in the sorority house, but the cycle started all over again. Within a month she looked emaciated, and began passing out in class. She had to be hospitalized again several more times that year.

Before the school year ended, Katrina had missed so much school that she was forced to drop out and move home. The next year I heard she was doing better. She enrolled in a different school because she had to live at home where her parents could watch her.

DEBT

While Greeks often go to great lengths for the perfect body, they also are surrounded by enormous pressure to keep up with the latest fashions, no matter how expensive.

Members of both fraternities and sororities must spend much of their time and money finding and buying the appropriate apparel for the countless parties. A new outfit, costume, formal dress, or tuxedo is usually required for each event. Typically, jewelry, flowers, and limousines are also part of the arrangement.

Clearly, debt is a less dangerous result of the never ending quest to fit the ideal image—less dangerous than, say, surgery or developing an eating disorder. However, it deserves mention because these events, complete with their companion protocol, are required. Greek members can, and often do, dig deep financial holes for themselves just trying to keep up with all the "necessities" expected.

"It is so hectic trying to keep up with all the formals and date parties that I finally just bought a tux on my credit card, because I had rented one so many times," recalled a fraternity member. "Then there are the corsages, the dinners before, the drinks at the party, the limos, the thank-you flowers, and, hopefully, the hotel room."

A sorority member admitted that she went into massive credit-card debt because she felt pressured to buy the most expensive designer garments. "People would usually ask where I bought anything I wore or who made it. When most of the girls wore Chanel makeup and Rolex watches, you were certainly going to do all that you could to not be wearing Revlon makeup and a Seiko watch."

I got into credit-card debt by attending all of the Greek trips—skiing in Tahoe, football games at Notre Dame or San Francisco, spring break in Mexico or Hawaii, and countless weekends in Catalina, Las Vegas, or Palm Springs. Each trip required a new swimming suit or ski outfit, hotel rooms, dinners out, plane tickets, and much, much more. While I had a lot of fun, the unfortunate part of these vacations was that most of us were so drunk all the time that we hardly remembered what we did.

Certainly, not every Greek student falls into these traps, but the overall mindset of the Greek system is to make "fitting in" the highest priority. For the most part, Greek students will easily charge on their credit card if they think it will win the approval of their fellow Greeks as well as that of the opposite sex. This creates a never ending cycle of fitting the ideal image, no matter what the cost or the consequence. Soon, those caught in the trap become so focused on the image that they lose their own identity, even forgetting why they are in college. In the end, they sacrifice themselves trying to attain the unattainable.

THE SOLUTION

In certain circles, the notion of physical perfection and its problematic effects upon young people is gaining some attention, particularly the use of steroids among boys and young men, and the profusion of eating disorders among girls and young women. Likewise, the link between unrealistic images of beauty presented in the media and the high frequency of distorted body images among young people is being solidified. However, much of the research and education to assuage this ever growing problem is aimed at youngsters, rather than college-age students; it is aimed at preventing, rather than rectifying, the problem.

Thus, a generation of young people today are left to sort through such unrealistic ideals and materialism themselves, armed only with perceptions gleaned from years of watching the rich, handsome man get the woman, and the sexy, beautiful woman get the man, on their television sets and movie screens.

Amazingly, Greek organizations have not considered this problem of doing whatever is necessary to fit in enough of a concern to look into, much less institute, a new approach. This problem particularly affects rushees and pledges, because they seem to be more worried about what others think of them and are easier to influence, than older members.

While such stereotyping and unrealistic physical images are addressed through media and women's studies classes on college campuses nationwide, there is much the Greek system itself can do to encourage students to adopt more responsible—more realistic—images of themselves and of others. One such measure is to require Greek students to enroll in such classes.

For instance, if rush were kept informal, students' first experience to the Greek system would be less materialistic. Rushees might not be as concerned about whether or not their outfit matched the established style of a particular sorority or fraternity. Similarly, if some of the formal and semiformal parties were replaced by casual parties, Greek students might feel less pressure to spend so much money on exorbitant outfits and accessories.

Likewise, if pledges were immediately considered new members, rather then pledges, they would probably feel more at ease being themselves and less pressure to conform.

As for the ideal image for men's and women's bodies that is so pervasive in the Greek system, change will be more difficult. But there are some measures Greek administrators can take, such as recognizing and banning anything sexist, both in fraternity and sorority events (contests and relays) and in chapter houses (posters, advertising, pornography, and so on).

LEARNING TO BE YOURSELF

It is understandable that students who suddenly find themselves in a new environment, with a newfound independence, often get wrapped up in trying to fit the mold of their Greek brothers or sisters. After all, it is easier to follow a large crowd with an established image than to maintain or create your own. But students who conform often regret that they wasted so much time and energy trying to be like someone else, trying to fit the mold.

College goes by very quickly, and it is an excellent time for students to gain an understanding of themselves. Just as adolescence is a time to question and test the boundaries of your parents, college is a time to discover your own boundaries, your vision and philosophy of life. It is through this quest that students gain the philosophical and emotional foundation that carries them through the next phase of life: adulthood.

THE PERFECT GREEK IMAGE

By conforming to the ideal image others hold, you are only hindering your own process of self-discovery—a process you will need to learn eventually. It's up to you: discover who you are now, or later.

8
RIVALRY

My friends and I were at our second fraternity party of the night, listening to music and talking in an upstairs room. We had locked the door to help keep our part of the party under control. Suddenly, someone started yelling and pounding on the door. When we recognized the voices of two football players we knew, we opened the door right away. They rushed in, desperate and out of breath.

"They're beating up Dave—we have to get them!" One of the guys hurriedly explained that members of the chief rival fraternity were picking a fight. We all rushed out the door, the guys gearing up for battle.

By the time I got there, about twenty guys were in the middle of a huge fistfight, all beating each other up. I was sickened by the sight of fists smacking into stomachs, legs kicking at bodies on the ground, and faces being slammed into each other. I knew the two fraternities had a long history of tension, but this was unbelievable. It was more the scene of street gangs pummeling each other in parking lots than a group of educated, and supposedly sophisticated, fraternity brothers.

Moments later, three police cars and an ambulance pulled up to the scene. As the police hustled out of their cars and onto the fraternity lawn, the crowd quickly dispersed, except for a small group of guys who had to be pulled apart.

I soon noticed that a friend of mine, Dave, was being put on a stretcher and carried to the ambulance. Running up to look at him, I saw that his eyes were closed and his head was bleeding. His girlfriend stood next to him, crying. He had never been the violent type, so I couldn't understand how this had happened. I later learned he'd been knocked unconscious, then battered and kicked several times while on the ground.

Helicopters began circling, with spotlights flashing down on us. The street was filled with people trying to get a closer look while the cops took down names and reports. Shaken and in a daze, I had to get away from the bloody scene. I quickly began walking to my sorority house.

It wasn't the first time that something so terrible had happened. The year before, the rival fraternity had been under investigation for two other beatings in which the victims almost lost their eyesight.

The newspaper reported that the fight had started when Dave was ordered not to walk in front of the opposing fraternity house, but this story differed from that of eyewitnesses. Another friend of mine, John, had been across the street with a fraternity brother when the fight began. He said it began when three men from the other fraternity started yelling rude comments to Dave's girlfriend as the couple walked past.

When Dave began to approach them, John said he heard the three rival fraternity members threaten Dave. "Don't —— come over here, or we'll kick the —— out of you!" they yelled.

Ignoring their threats, Dave kept approaching. For about ten seconds, the guys yelled back and forth at each other until one of them punched Dave. He immediately fell down, unconscious, yet they continued to beat him. That's when John and his friend ran across the street to defend Dave. Gradually, more and more guys from both fraternities saw the fight and joined in, until it turned into the violent uproar I had seen.

Such brutal fights among Greeks are not isolated incidents; they happen regularly on campuses across the nation. The rivalry between some sororities and fraternities can be so severe that the tension develops into serious physical confrontations and even near riots. In addition to suffering physical injuries, Greeks and other students may have the course of their lives indelibly altered with arrests or even imprisonment as a result of such ruthless fights.

QUARRELING

Fights between sororities are also common, but are usually more verbal than physical. Generally, these disagreements are meaningless arguments about trivial topics, but sometimes they stem from deep-seated jealousy and competition.

One time when I was a Little Sister, I was waiting in line with two other Little Sisters to use the bathroom. All at once, a short, blonde woman from another sorority walked right past us, got in the front of the line, and quickly went into a stall. My friend Kelly was furious. Her alcohol consumption made her more assertive than usual, and she began rudely blaming the woman's sorority for her attitude.

"Sure, just cut in line!" she fumed. "That's right, you're in the —— sorority, so you have the right to be rude and obnoxious. You think you're something special, but have you looked at how fat you and all of your sorority sisters' butts are? I'm actually amazed that you could squeeze through here at all!"

The woman stepped out of the stall and right up to Kelly, who towered over her.

"You just wish you could wear our letters, because your boyfriend likes our sorority sisters better than you!" Then, before Kelly could react, the woman reached up and slapped Kelly and stormed out of the bathroom.

The other women in the bathroom let out an "ooooh!" as Kelly stood there with her mouth wide open, amazed. To her credit, Kelly ignored what happened to prevent the conflict from spiraling out of control.

This kind of contention is widespread between Little Sisters as well. One fraternity member said that although he had never seen his Little Sisters fighting with fists, he frequently saw "cat fights" and bickering over guys.

"They get a little drunk and make fools out of themselves," he said. "It's probably stuff they would never do when sober, unless they were really enraged. But if you're a little buzzed, you don't care how you look or if you're making a fool out of yourself. That's when they'd make a bigger deal out of nothing. I've seen that a lot."

FIGHTING

Rivalry between fraternities and sororities is nothing new. For as long as they've been around, fraternities and sororities have competed with one another over grade-point averages, popularity, and having the best parties. Oftentimes, Greek houses are encouraged to compete, through organized events such as contests and relay races.

The rivalry that used to be seen in harmless pranks between houses, however, has seemingly escalated into an all-out war. In fraternities, these wars are fought in life-threatening, gang-type fights such as the one I witnessed, as well as smaller scuffles between four to eight fraternity men. According to an insurance company's five-year study on fraternities, said Jonathan Brant, an advisor from the National Interfraternity Conference, "next to accidents, fighting was the next most common reason for a claim."

I saw these smaller conflicts just about every other weekend at public places where all the fraternity and sorority members would gather, such as bars, college concerts, or sports events. (Rarely would such a disturbance occur at fraternity houses, because rival members were purposely not invited in.) All too often, fun evenings were interrupted or ended because of some-one starting a brawl. The young men involved usually ended up with bloody noses and cuts.

One fraternity member admitted that such hotheaded behav-ior often got out of hand.

"When you get in a fight, you don't think you could serious-ly hurt or kill someone," he said. "You never stop and think, 'This guy is unconscious; I shouldn't be hitting him anymore.' You're so pissed off, you're not thinking."

As I look back on all the fights I witnessed, never do I recall one starting because of an important dispute.

"They would always start over something absolutely stupid, like talking to a girl or somebody spilling a beer on somebody," recalled a fraternity member. "With the exception of a few, every fight I saw would always start with just two people and end up with a whole bunch of people hitting a bunch of other people."

Fighting is not reserved solely for rivals, however. Skirmishes often break out between friends as well, including brothers from the same fraternity. Once, while I was walking home with a group of friends, my boyfriend became enraged when one of his fraternity brothers monopolized the conversation with me. Suddenly he pushed the guy from behind, knocking him down into some bushes. Fortunately, the other fraternity brothers in the group quickly separated the two before any real damage was done.

Another fraternity member, whom I'll call Rick, told how he got into a fight when a guy from a different house accidentally spilled beer on him. When Rick demanded an apology, the rival refused. Rick tried to cool down, but when the other guy spit out a string of profanities, Rick couldn't take it.

Enraged, Rick slugged his opponent as hard as he could. Even when the guy fell down unconscious, Rick was so angry that he kept hitting and kicking him in the head.

Only when another fraternity brother pulled Rick off and

held him down did he stop. In the end, Rick and his friends carried the guy to his fraternity house, threw him into the bushes, and left him there, bloody and unconscious.

ARRESTS

These terrible fights often result in arrests. One of the men involved in the huge fight that I witnessed was arrested—his third offense in such incidents.

In September 1995, San Diego County's Superior Court Judge told twenty-year-old Derek and twenty-one-year-old Nam that a year should be the minimum time spent behind bars, followed by five years of supervised probation. These young men pleaded guilty to one count of mayhem for their part in the beating of two nineteen-year-old men at San Onofre State Beach.

The attack erupted after the victims, who were camping with their girlfriends, asked a group of a dozen or more students at the next campsight (most of them members of a fraternity at San Diego State University) to turn down their music, since it was almost midnight. One of the victims said he was initially attacked by one male, but soon others joined in, slamming his head into his parked truck. Another attacker grabbed his penis through his sweat pants, then squeezed and wrenched it from side to side. The other victim's attacker tried to strangle him while he was being kicked and punched. This victim ended up with a swollen head, swollen shut eyes, beaten ribs, and one of his shoulders knocked out of its socket. The other victim now has a plate in his head.

A fight at Radford University in Virginia involved five members from two rival fraternities who were arrested afterwards and charged with felonies. The fight left two members in need of medical treatment.[1]

At the University of Nebraska-Kearney, a fight broke out at a fraternity party where one student was charged with two counts of third-degree assault, two others with disorderly conduct, and a fourth with being a minor in possession after police found him passed out in a nearby vehicle.[2]

While not often publicized, this kind of behavior is common in the Greek system. And it perpetuates itself. One man hits another, another joins in, and another, and so on. By reacting with rage and violence, a pattern is set—a pattern that could stay with these men throughout their lives.

THE SYSTEM

It is the structure of the Greek system that supports the competitive tension that so often leads to extreme hostility between sororities and fraternities.

Most agree that this competition begins with the recruitment process. As mentioned in previous chapters, rush is the time when individual sororities and fraternities focus exclusively on convincing rushees that their house is better than the others, attempting to persuade the most desirable students to join. The tension can become so strong that the resentful feelings developed between houses during rush that last the entire year.

When I was participating in my sorority's rush campaign, the rush chairman announced each morning how we compared with the other sororities, from the most popular to the least popular, based on computer-generated results of the selection cards turned in by rushees at the end of the previous day. Our rating was a source of much anxiety and stress for each of us, so we listened closely for the results. Any sorority that ranked higher than ours was hated, and if we did poorly, the chairman would scold us for not doing better.

"I can't believe we are letting the other houses get these girls!" she would say. "Our house is going to be ruined if you don't do something about it today!"

Then, full of new resolve, we would go out to beat the competition by recruiting the best rushees for our house.

Inevitably, there is always someone who is wanted by a certain sorority or fraternity but who ends up pledging another house. Throughout the rest of the school year, seeing the pledge who "got away" wearing the pin or T-shirt of the rival house reminds the members of their loss, and fires them up for the next competition.

"We'd think, 'I hope that pledge regrets that he chose their house over ours,'" a fraternity member said. "Then you just want to get back at the other fraternity for pledging the guy that your house really wanted."

More rivalry and resentment are created if a house's ranking goes down because of the success of another fraternity or sorority. Often when a sorority or fraternity house performs poorly during rush, the members find that their image—a sacred commodity, as already discussed—has changed. Their hostility escalates as they find they aren't being invited to parties with the top houses, houses they socialized with the year before.

One year something similar happened in my sorority. It was a long-standing tradition: we were always invited to a specific annual party hosted by a popular fraternity. That is, until this year. Instead of inviting our house, they invited another sorority which, according to the rating results, had a better rush. The rest of that year, we viciously resented the other house, an ongoing rivalry that frequently resulted in shouting matches.

After individuals become pledges and then members, they are usually taught to have pride in their organization, and to always show loyalty to its members. While there is nothing wrong with that, these ideas are often carried to extremes, fostering the idea that theirs must be the best organization, making others inferior.

A 1989 study of competition and superiority within fraternities resulted in the following conclusion:

> Interfraternity rivalry fosters in-group identification and out-group hostility. Fraternities stress pride of membership and superiority over other fraternities as major

goals. Interfraternity rivalries take many forms, including competition for desirable pledges, size of pledge class, size of membership, size and appearance of fraternity houses, superiority in intramural sports, highest grade-point averages, giving the best parties, gaining the best or most campus leadership roles, and, of great importance, attracting and displaying "good-looking women."[3]

One fraternity member explained that labeling certain groups to be all one way or the other contributes to the hostility.

"The Greek system promotes stuff like that because of pride," he said. "You are told as a pledge that all the other houses are losers, and your house is the best, no matter what house you're in."

He added that members in every house constantly label the other groups with derogatory stereotypes, programming their brothers toward prejudice and hate, and eventually leading to vicious fights.

"Even though you might meet some of the other fraternity members in your classes and like them, you would still stereotype the fraternity they were in, and would take any opportunity to beat them up," he said.

Another fraternity member explained why he believes the rivalry between houses continues to be a tradition.

"The older guys instill in the younger guys that we are the best, and we are taught that if any of the other fraternities have a problem with us, we should beat them up," he said. "The newer members are so vulnerable and young that they are easily brainwashed into believing that fighting the other fraternities is cool.

"If we were told to be cool to the other fraternities and invite them to all of our parties, then that's what we would've done."

Clearly, Greek students sometimes put pride in their fraterni-

ty or sorority ahead of common sense. It's continually empha-
sized that members should have so much pride in their sisters or
brothers that they should be willing to do anything for them,
supporting them whatever the situation might be. Such blind
loyalty can lead to vicious fights.

"You tend to back up your brothers, even if it's a brother
you don't like or you wouldn't back up if he weren't your bro,"
one fraternity member said. "There were many guys who I
thought were dorks—but because they were my bros, I would
back them up if they got into a fight."

SPORTS

Throughout the year, all the Greek houses participate in organized sports competitions, pitting fraternities against fraternities
and sororities against sororities. The year is filled with events
such as football, Ping-Pong, volleyball, basketball, softball, tennis—just about any sporting event that exists. On the surface,
this appears a great idea, but playing in such highly publicized,
intense competitions for trophies and other prizes only adds to
the fierce rivalry between houses.

"When I play in the intersorority competition, I get really
aggressive, because I want our house to win so bad," said one
sports-minded sorority member. She added that she wanted to
win because of the recognition it would give her sorority.

"Sometimes it gets a lot rougher than when I'm just playing
with my friends. We [rival sororities] hate each other so much
that we end up trying to hurt each other."

She added that much of the hatred between the groups is
already well established before such sports events take place.

"There is always some girl in another house who stole your
friend's boyfriend, or who is trying to," she said. "Or, you might
hate them because they were invited to a fraternity party that
your house wanted to go to, but was not asked—things like
that."

A fraternity member agreed that sports events merely add to

the existing competition. They are important to most fraternity and sorority houses because each group wants to win the "bragging rights," allowing them to appear superior to the others. Winning a sports competition is just another opportunity for the organization to put down the other groups as losers.

JEALOUSY

Bitter sparks also fly between rival fraternities and sororities when jealousy of the opposite sex is involved. Greek students take great pride in who is on their arm, because of the status they will enjoy by dating someone popular. It's no wonder, then, that competitive tension explodes when two or more opposing members want to date the same popular person.

As large as some colleges are, there never seems to be enough popular individuals available to date, especially when many sororities or fraternities schedule their date parties on the same weekends. These date parties are formal, semiformal, or costume parties which inevitably create another form of competition among the houses. For these weekends, all of the fraternity or sorority members are trying to get the best-looking, most popular date. So serious strife can arise when someone asks out a rival's potential date first.

One sorority member told of a serious fight she felt responsible for starting. Just before her sorority's annual formal, Brittany broke up with Ken, her boyfriend of six months, after learning he had cheated on her. Even though Ken persisted in calling her and begging her forgiveness, Brittany asked another guy to the formal.

But Ken wouldn't give up. Without Brittany's knowledge, he went to the formal with a woman from the sorority cosponsoring the party.

Brittany didn't realize that Ken was at the party until he was an inch away from her date's face, yelling profanities.

"In only a couple of seconds, he was punching my date in

the stomach," she said. "Thank God, there were lots of my date's fraternity brothers there to help him, because he got beaten up pretty good."

That wasn't the end, however. After the fight, her date's fraternity brothers took Ken outside and beat him up, too. The evening was a disaster.

Friction over the opposite sex even happens among brothers who belong to the same fraternity. One fraternity member grew enraged when he discovered that the woman he had asked to a date party was making out with one of his fraternity brothers in his room. A nasty fight ensued between the two brothers.

Because the lives of Greek members are so intertwined, bitter resentments and jealousy also linger among Greeks who have dated and then broken up, for whatever reason. Friction often occurs at Greek parties when former couples run into each other, especially when someone new is on their arm.

THE ALCOHOL LINK

Alcohol and drugs, which are imbedded in Greek culture, also contribute greatly to the fighting that breaks out among Greek members. One fraternity brother reported that alcohol was the primary reason fraternity members fight.

"Guys look for an excuse to fight when they are drunk," he said, adding that when he is sober, he may not even think about fighting someone from an opposing fraternity. "But when you're drunk, your emotions tend to be exaggerated. Then when someone makes you mad, it's like, 'Those damn —— , let's kick their butts!' So I think alcohol has something to do with it about 90 percent of the time."

"Fighting, like most of these issues [sexual harassment, rape, and so on], relates to alcohol," said a member of the National Interfraternity Conference, referring to physical confrontation and other problems within the Greek system. "When someone is under the influence of alcohol, they often act very differently than they would under normal circumstances."

SOME POSSIBLE CURES

There are ways to discourage Greeks from being hostile toward each other—ways that should seriously be considered by national Greek organizations. For example, if Greek students were to form competitive teams comprising members from several houses, the all-important stakes of house identity and image would be lowered. Plus, Greek students would likely establish friendships with members from other houses.

Likewise, if sororities and fraternities were required to invite and host parties with other sororities and fraternities, the competition between individual houses would likely be lessened. Such a policy would not only ensure that all sororities and fraternities were invited to the "best" parties, but also douse the fiery competition over recruiting the best-looking pledges during rush each year.

Along the same lines, Greek administers could pre-assign a list of fraternities and sororities to be paired throughout the school year. To prevent the formation of a pair identity, fraternity-sorority combinations would have to be rotated year after year, until all houses had been paired with one another.

A less-structural solution would be to encourage individual houses to build a rapport with one another through programming offered by the national Greek organizations and universities. The National Panhellenic Conference already encourages Greek organizations to help one another and their community through its"Panhellenic Spirit" program. The most recent example of Panhellenic Spirit took place on the University of Southern California campus, where the successful sorority Phi Beta Pi helped a new struggling sorority, Alpha Epsilon Phi, with rush, showing them how to greet rushees, perform skits, and generally organize rush procedures.

Bitter rivalry tears away at the very foundation of the Greek system. Competition can be healthy, but becoming obsessed with having a better reputation than other Greek organizations—to the point of risking the safety of others—is senseless.

Clearly, Greek organizations need to encourage cooperation, rather than competition, between individual houses. Before rivalry can become a thing of the past, however, the traditional Greek mindset must change. New and old members alike should be encouraged to feel pride in themselves and in the Greek organization as a whole.

9
RACISM

I shifted uncomfortably in my seat, trying to plot a tactful escape. After a night at a local bar with a group of fraternity and sorority members, I had joined them for a late-night dinner at a nearby Mexican restaurant. Most in our group were very drunk, and the conversation had turned ugly. One fraternity brother, known for his racist comments, was spreading a malicious rumor about one of the few black fraternity guys.

That week was African-American Week on campus, the annual recognition of the accomplishments of African-Americans, and Jim minced no words in cutting down everything the week was about. For the most part, I had always thought Jim overbearing and bigoted, but it was especially annoying that he assumed everyone was as bigoted as he.

As Jim continued spewing racial slurs and cutting down a sorority member for dating a racially mixed fraternity brother, I sat there thinking of everything I wanted to say—but fear held my tongue. I knew that if I said anything, Jim and the others would start a rumor about me, as well. Besides, the guys in the group were all quite large, and I was afraid of what they might do to me.

Jim's name calling soon evolved into hateful comments about blacks in general, and some of the others began joining in. Then, all at once, the conversation turned from general malice to planning a specific attack on African-Americans.

I had to get out of there, but how could I leave without causing suspicion?

"Oh, I forgot my credit card at the bar!" I said suddenly. "I have to go back and get it."

Hoping no one would remember that I'd been buying drinks with cash all night, I hurried out of the bar before anyone could stop me. I could only guess what was going to happen, but I didn't want to stick around to find out.

The next day, two of the women who had been at the bar came to my room to see if I'd made it home. One of them had gone back to the bar looking for me, but couldn't find me.

"You missed out on such a fun night!" they said, and began recounting the so-called exciting events.

For their own tribute to African-American Week, the fraternity guys at the table had decided to beat up a black student they'd seen at the bar earlier that night. They had watched and waited at the restaurant until they saw him leave, and then had followed him down a secluded alley. Seeing their chance, the guys rushed up and began punching him in the stomach while the women watched. When he fell down, they each gave him a few swift kicks before running off, leaving him curled up on the ground.

I could not believe what I was hearing. I wasn't sure who the black student was, but I felt sorry for him—and I began to wonder how often this kind of thing happened. I thought about telling someone in the school administration, but because I hadn't been there and wasn't even sure who the victim was, I knew nothing would come of it.

Incidents like these, coupled with much research, provide overwhelming proof that the Greek system discriminates against minorities and perpetuates segregation. One study describes established patterns of Greek stereotyping and racial violence toward minorities[1] while another states that "fraternities and sororities cannot be defined as bastions of tolerance when it comes to minority differences."[2] Most recently, a study found that sororities discourage African-American women from trying to become members of their house.[3]

Looking into the foundation of the Greek system, it's easy to see how racism began. Before the civil rights movement in the 1960s, most fraternities and sororities had rules forbidding them to pledge any member who wasn't white. Since 1963, Greek organizations have been required by federal law not to discriminate on the basis of race. Yet today, more than thirty years later, the Greek system is still predominantly white and racially segregated, with almost no interaction between the groups. Blacks and whites have separate organizations with different governing structures.[4]

ORGANIZED RACIST EVENTS

Each year, college Greek organizations all over the nation actively participate in ethnically offensive or racist events.

• In 1988, at Oklahoma State University, members of a predominantly white fraternity "dressed up as black slaves and serenaded sorority houses during a "plantation party."[5]

• In 1985, a University of Cincinnati fraternity was suspended for two years following a Martin Luther King, Jr., "trash party." The members allegedly asked guests to bring Ku Klux Klan hoods, canceled welfare checks, radios "as big as your head," and "your father, if you know who he is."[6]

• In 1988, at Arizona State University, a fraternity was suspended for two years following several instances of abuse, including forcing Jewish pledges to recite, "My number is six million. That's how many Jews were killed [in the holocaust] and I should have been one of them, sir."[7]

• In January 1993, a fraternity at Rider College in

Lawrenceville, New Jersey, had a "Dress Like a Nigger Night." Pledges were told to dress in baggy clothes, speak in stereotypical black speech, and paint Xs on their foreheads (to symbolize Malcolm X) for a cleaning session at the chapter house.[8]

• In April 1991 at George Mason University in Richmond, Virginia, a fraternity had an "ugly-woman contest" featuring one member who came with a painted black face, a black wig with curlers, and an outfit stuffed with pillows to simulate large buttocks and breasts. He spoke in slang to parody blacks.[9]

• In April 1995, at William Jewell University in Kansas City, Missouri, one fraternity outraged black students and the administration by dressing in supposed medieval garb very similar to robes worn by the Ku Klux Klan. They marched in these uniforms through the dormitories in an attempt to find "fair maidens" to accompany them to a party. Ensuing tension over the incident advanced into racial slurs and threats toward some black students.[10]

• In October 1992, a fraternity songbook with obscene racist songs was discovered at the University of California-Los Angeles. Some of the lyrics were about a "hot . . . Mexican whore" who still had strong sexual desires even in her grave, "while maggots crawl out of her decomposed womb." Another song called rival fraternity members "dirty . . . fags" who "contracted AIDS and died."[11]

In my own interviews, a few sorority members admitted to participating in accounts of blatant prejudice toward the only Jewish sorority on campus. "We had been partying and someone started calling the Jewish sorority all kinds of names and saying they didn't belong on the row," one said. "She quickly convinced us that we should give them a good scare." Another admitted that she and a group from her sorority used paint and brushes from their sorority house to paint a swastika on the sidewalk in front of the Jewish sorority house.

The problem of racism in the Greek system is difficult for college administrations to correct, despite the fact that many campuses have racial harassment policies against stigmatizing or victimizing individuals on the basis of race or ethnicity. Greek organizations argue that they have the constitutional right of freedom of speech to hold events that promote racial or ethnic biases. And because they lack the resources for costly trial expenses, unlike Greek organizations, most universities cannot pursue punishment in court.

RACE WARS

Fights and racial slurs often arise when black and white Greek organizations are together at the same parties or events. Racism becomes evident when blacks and whites are actually slugging one another over their prejudices.

I witnessed many fights that started over racial hostilities. Black and white organizations gathered together so rarely that the prejudiced attitudes of many white members were obvious: Not only did they consider themselves superior to those in black organizations, they often seemed to think blacks shouldn't be allowed to attend popular campus events.

For example, one semester I was surprised to see many blacks attending an open party when there were only a few blacks in the Greek system at that time. Seemingly, things were going well, blacks and whites mixing together and having a good time. "This is great," I said to myself, "we should have more parties like this—"

I spoke too soon. One of the white fraternity members began yelling racial slurs at a black fraternity member, and a huge fight broke out. I ran for safety, and campus security finally broke up the fight.

Not all racial fights are on such a small scale, however; nor are they as easily quashed. In 1994, an Illinois State University student who had been involved in an earlier racially charged confrontation with police was again arrested for allegedly beating a man in an interfraternity brawl. The fight included small scuffles and beatings that began an hour after rival fraternity members arrived at the dance chanting and yelling profanities.[12]

In 1995, the University of Memphis chapter of the Kappa Alpha fraternity was shut down after a weekend fight. Members of the all-white fraternity got into a fight with three junior transfer students—one white and two black. Racial slurs and blows were exchanged. The brawl triggered another incident of interracial violence just days later, which left the Kappa Alpha rush chairman with injuries that required stitches.[13]

Also in 1995, the University of Arkansas chapter of the Sigma Epsilon Phi fraternity was suspended by its national chapter after members were accused of yelling racial epithets and throwing a chair at a black professor who was trying to photograph a racist statue in front of their fraternity house.[14]

Clearly, such racial tension springs from the unhealthy attitudes of racial prejudice so prevalent in the Greek system. In my experience, cruel racial slurs and jokes made in passing were so common that I thought those saying them were joking. Not until I began interviewing Greek members for this book did I realize that they actually believed such statements were true.

One sorority member explained why she believes blacks and whites shouldn't belong to the same organizations: "I just think they are better off with their own kind. They dress, talk, and act so different from us, that it's hard for us to hang out together." She went on to say that she hated to see interracial dating, and that mixing blacks and whites together in social clubs would only promote more of that sort of thing.

A fraternity member also told of his opposition to integrating the Greek system: "I don't think we should be in the same fraternities and sororities because we are too different—they listen to rap and are into gang bangs, funky clothes, and souped-up cars. They are just into their own thing and it's better that way. Besides, I don't trust them."

I began to understand some of the difficulty minorities face in the predominantly white Greek system when I tried to fix up a black pledge sister with a date. A couple of fraternity brothers had begged me to fix them up with dates for an upcoming party, and the women I had in mind were both so fun and attractive I was sure I was doing these guys a favor. But as soon as they found out one of the women was black, they refused.

"Whoever takes her out will never hear the end of it," one of them explained. "We'll be harassed for the rest of our lives, and it's not worth it. Besides, I could never kiss someone black. That is just sick!"

Another fraternity member in the room put in his two cents. "You can't expect anyone to go out with your pledge sister," he said. "She is just going to have to realize that if she wants to be in *our* Greek system, she is never going to get any dates."

I was furious, and spent the next few hours trying to convince the guys how wrong they were. Ultimately, they agreed to take the women to the party as friends, but the two women were left to hang out at the party by themselves.

I never told my friend what difficulty I had getting her that date, but a few years later at a Greek ski trip, she confided a little of her daily struggles as a minority in the Greek system.

"I am so sick of people and their racial joking," she said as we got ready to go out for the evening. "Jack was just going on and on about how he can't stand blacks. I mean, what does he think *I* am? He was saying all these mean things to everyone, as if I were not even there. I have heard so much of it on this whole trip, I'm fed up with it!"

I didn't know what to say. I could tell it was too painful and embarrassing for her to go into detail. I tried to reassure her that Jack hadn't meant to hurt her feelings, but I could only hope that what I said was true.

DISCRIMINATION

All too often, the elite system of rush discourages minorities from joining the Greek system. One woman admitted that there were always a few in her sorority who didn't want minorities to join, and would do whatever they could to keep them from joining.

"Our house never even had to vote on any minority women," said another. "There were always so few of them rushing, and those who did, we never even considered."

A sorority member related what she and her friends told blacks to deter them from becoming interested in their sorority. "We usually date white boys and have functions with white people," she and her sorority sisters would say. "Did you know there is also a black Greek system? Do you know about it?"[15]

"I've never had a positive experience," said one black sorority member. "I went through rush two years ago, and I was the only black girl in the house. Some people wanted me and others didn't, and I could feel it."[16]

"Black students have told me there are some fraternities they just can't get into," said Lad Sessions, a philosophy professor at Washington and Lee University in Lexington, Virginia.[17]

In 1994, researchers studied sorority integration at the university with the largest Greek system in the Southeast, the University of Florida. Out of seventeen recognized sororities, there were more than two thousand sorority members. Not one African-American lived in any of the sixteen white sorority houses, however. Most black women interested in joining the Greek system were encouraged to join one of the three black sororities, only one of which was recognized by the college. None of the three black sororities had houses.

Researchers also observed a preview presentation for incoming freshmen and their parents to introduce them to the campus and show them their first glimpse of the Greek organizations. Presented entirely by white sorority members, the preview featured a slide presentation depicting white women studying, playing sports, and partying together. Out of more than one hundred slides, only three depicted African-Americans—two group pictures of an all-black sorority and one picture of a black woman and a white woman hugging.[18]

I found the Greek system on the West Coast to be equally segregated. One woman in my sorority was half-black, and another was part Asian—but no full-blooded minorities of any kind were members.

As has already been discussed, image and reputation are of the utmost importance to sororities and fraternities. It seems that Greeks tend to believe that if they accept black members, it will lower their prestige and reputation on campus.

Indeed, it is usually the less-popular sororities that accept minority rushees. Because these houses often have a hard time recruiting members—without enough members to pay the bills, they would have to shut down—they usually accept whoever wants to join just to stay afloat.

"Frankly, my sorority is not a very desirable sorority to be in socially. We just aren't," admitted one sorority member. "Because we are not all beauty queens, we are probably more flexible [about minorities]. If we were more popular, I am sure that would change. Let's face it—sororities are social and exclusive, and that is that."

"I certainly think the discrimination is there," agreed another sorority member. "I think the better [more popular] chapters feel that they cannot risk their image."[19]

A fraternity member who was Jewish described how perpetual ridicule chipped away at his self-worth. "There are a couple other guys in the house that are Jewish, and we get harassed all the time," he said. "I've been called every insulting name you could think of regarding being Jewish. We always just laugh it off."

A partially Korean sorority member said she was hazed much more as a pledge, and often felt left out even after becoming a member. "I know the girls in my house who think I'm ruining the house's reputation," she said. "They have tried so hard since the day I was accepted to get me to drop out."

THE RATIONALE

White fraternity and sorority members give many excuses for the obvious racial separation in the Greek system. In 1994, after conducting a study on segregation in sororities, researchers reported that when they began interviewing sorority members, they quickly realized they were not the first to question their exclusionary policies.

"We make it a policy not to talk about that," one member told them.

"We have been told [by our sorority] to say that [segregation] is entirely by choice," another answered with hostility.

Yet another hinted that she knew what her sorority was doing was wrong: "I don't want to get in trouble [by talking to you]."

When the researchers tried to get some statistics on segregation for their study, a chapter alumnus advisor acted as if the problem didn't even exist, saying, "We are unable to provide you with a racial background. We do not consider . . . the racial or religious background of any of our members, therefore, we do not have access to this information."

White sorority members frequently told researchers that blacks preferred the status quo of segregation, and that recruiting African-American women would anger the black sororities. "I do not think the blacks want to integrate the system any more than we do," said one.[20]

When I asked Greeks to explain this situation during my own research, I found that most tried to convince me that the blacks were responsible for the segregation, claiming that because blacks had created their own fraternity and sorority system, that's the one they should join.

"They have their own houses, so why would they want to belong to ours?" one sorority member rationalized.

Some students went so far as to blame racial tension on black students. "They hang out together on campus in their own area and never get close enough to talk to anyone else," said one fraternity member. "If they never make any effort to integrate, they must not want to, so why should [white Greeks]?"

On the surface, it might appear that way. At my own college, minority organizations always stuck together. At all-school events such as sports, black students sat together in one section of the seats, while we whites sat in another. Clearly, however, blaming minorities for segregation is nonsense. It is in reacting to being pushed out and discriminated against that most minorities form their own organizations. After all, how long should a group of people fight to prove their equality and worth to others who aren't willing to listen?

The rules of the Greek system no longer forbid blacks, Jews, and other minorities from becoming members, yet it seems that many organizations continue to discriminate. For example, many colleges and universities are recruiting more and more students of different racial backgrounds, yet many fraternities and sororities have not changed much in their recruitment process to attract these students. Researchers concluded, in the 1994 study at the University of Florida, that rush needed to be restructured before minorities would feel encouraged to join. "Evidence demonstrates that the social structure of Greek segregation in this setting is self-perpetuating," they said. "Although racial prejudice is a factor in the systematic exclusion of minorities, the root causes of racial separation are systemic and endemic to the . . . recruitment process itself. Even those . . . who want to change the system are powerless in the face of a recruitment structure that subverts integration."[21]

Some Greek advisors argue, the reason minorities do not feel encouraged to join the general Greek organizations is that they do not see themselves reflected in the same percentage as whites in existing houses. Which, they add, is because the percentage of minorities was not as large four or five years ago, when the resource pool of minority students may have been smaller than it is today. A member of the National Panhellenic Council said, "It is going to take some time before the percentages equal out, if they ever do."

Advisors also report that this underrepresentation is more of a concern in certain regions of the country. On a college campus in Maine, for example, there are probably only a few Asian students, representing a very small percentage of total students, whereas on some campuses in southern California, that number is more than 50 percent.

On primarily white college campuses, black fraternities and sororities usually provide the major social structure for all black students on campus, both Greek and non-Greek students. In contrast, the predominantly white Greek chapters usually hold social events solely for their own members, members of the other general Greek organizations, and invited guests.

The eight national predominantly black Greek organizations—four sororities and four fraternities—were formed to "provide a harbor for . . . members from hatred and isolation, to pull together the best-trained African-American minds, and to give leadership to the African-American community in its struggle for freedom and justice."[22]

As it turns out, white fraternities and sororities could learn from minority houses. Since the founding of the first black fraternity in 1906, Alpha Phi at Cornell University, black fraternities and sororities have proven to foster some important qualities in their members—qualities that all Greek organizations strive to instill in their membership.[23] In a 1989 study, Greek African-Americans were found to be more service-oriented and, compared to the white sororities and fraternities, black organizations had a much larger proportion of alumni who stay active with their campus chapters.

Unfortunately, there has been little research conducted regarding the values and attitudes of black Greeks over the last twenty years. A 1987 study, however, compared the values of black fraternity men to those of white fraternity men, and found that the blacks were more liberal, socially conscious, and culturally sophisticated than the whites.[24] In 1991, another study showed that black Greek members seem to place a higher value than do general Greek members on the development of peer independence, liberalism, social conscience, motivation for grades, and good study habits.[25]

ENCOURAGING DIVERSIFICATION

Segregation is deplorable anywhere. But it is especially bothersome at colleges and universities, where students are supposed to be gaining an education and a deeper understanding of their world, and of other cultures.

Although it will likely be uncomfortable for white students in the Greek system, who have been allowed, and even encouraged, to harbor such racial prejudice for so long, Greek organizations must begin to encourage minorities to join their groups. It is only in understanding and exposure that people learn to tolerate, and ultimately accept, people from different ethnic backgrounds.

Requiring sororities and fraternities to adhere to minority membership quotas might be one way to prevent discrimination in general fraternity and sorority rush procedures. Just as sororities place quotas on the number of new members each house can bid, quotas for the number of minorities going through rush could be enforced. This would probably prompt sororities and fraternities to think of innovative ways to attract and involve minorities in their events. One such way would be to invite minority members to take highly visible roles during rush, such as participating in skits, songs, slide shows, and other activities, and seek rush leadership positions.

Another way to reduce racism in the Greek system is for Greek advisors and university administrators to create more ways that all fraternity and sorority organizations, black and white, can interact positively with each other. These could be alcohol-free situations that encourage groups to mix together to possibly make friends with members from organizations other than their own.

Before integration can occur at social and other Greek events, however, the very heart of the Greek system must be addressed: the process of recruitment. The National Interfraternity Conference is in the midst of what will reportedly be a three-year effort to change the way members view recruitment and how they expect nonmembers to interact with them.

In the past, fraternities created barriers that would allow only those students who were interested to join a fraternity. They put up posters and handed out pamphlets (sometimes charging a fee) containing the details of a very formal rush. Such a formal rush excludes students who come to campus not knowing anything about the Greek system. This type of recruitment process made membership so difficult that only those students who knew about and passionately wanted to join a fraternity would clear those hurdles and go through the process.

Today, many minority college students are coming to campus as the first ones in their family to attend college, or, if their parents did go to college, they are likely the first ones to encounter Greek life. Many more are international students who have come from other countries where little, if anything, is known about the Greek system.

Because members of the National Interfraternity Conference felt they should be responsible for fraternities' systemic approach to recruitment, they created the fraternity form model. As an alternative to the traditional formal rush and recruitment process, this model encourages fraternities to get together and set up a circus tent in an exhibit area. Refreshments are provided and the location is central, such as near a parking lot or in the middle of campus, to attract a wide array of potential members. Because students do not have to go to a particular place or dress a certain way, this model approach provides an opportunity for students to meet many Greek members without being overwhelmed by a structure or the pressure to join. It is a one-on-one, people-meeting-people approach.

If fraternities choose to use this kind of interaction, rather than the traditional recruitment process, members of the National Interfraternity Conference believe that students from many different backgrounds, faiths, nations, and creeds may interact with one another and possibly join. Because of its own rules of organization, the council cannot dictate that every fraternity use the form model, so the choice lies with each individual house or campus. The council has a wide array of resources for those who choose the form model, including literature and other material, and students trained in executing such an approach. When it is used, the form model dramatically increases the number of people joining fraternities. It is not yet known whether the process is increasing the number of minorities who join, but it is definitely a positive approach toward embracing diversity—an approach both fraternities and sororities would be wise to try.

It is time for a serious change in the way people of minority races are treated within the Greek system. Like this country, most college campuses have become a melting pot of every ethnicity. Yet, the Greek system has maintained a predominantly Caucasian face. My hope is that after reviewing the information in this chapter, students will realize the necessity of accepting—or, even better, encouraging—minority integration among the general population of fraternities and sororities.

ΠΔΣΩΠΔΣΩΠΔΣΩΠΔΣΩΠΔΣΩΠΔΣ

AFTERWORD

I looked across the restaurant table at my sorority sisters, feeling as if no time had passed. We had been out of college for a couple of years now, and here we were, all grown up. Our transition from college into the real world now saw one of us directing a television show, another consulting for a cable company, one assisting the vice president of a large company, and another applying to graduate schools. And then there was I, the writer. Besides the usual catching up on our personal lives, the conversation centered around the topic of this book, the need to bring change in the Greek system.

"I can't believe we were so involved that we just ignored all the problems," one of my friends said. "Once we joined, our main goal was to be one of the classy girls."

The others nodded in agreement.

"I knew what was going on, but I was too worried about what other Greeks thought of me to say anything," said another.

I shook my head. "We were all that way," I said. "At least with this book, students can begin to recognize some of the real problems before they join—and maybe some changes will finally be made."

My friends were excited that through the book I could finally tell others what we should have had the nerve to disclose when we were in college. They agreed with me, that students should have a better understanding of the system that lies beneath the big, fake smiles they see at fraternity and sorority rush parties.

While sometimes it can appear that the Greek system is the main social structure on campus, there are many other clubs and organizations with the same potential for forming close friendships. Most colleges have clubs and activities such as student government, choral groups, concert band, drama clubs, dance companies, magazines, radio programs, student newspapers, yearbook clubs, volunteer organizations, minority clubs, jazz band, marching band, music ensembles, musical theater, opera, film and television clubs, symphony orchestra, religious clubs, honors groups, international clubs, leadership groups, and clubs for most majors. These groups offer unlimited potential for learning and forming friendships. The college dormitories are also a good way to make friends and to get involved in campus life. With such a wide array of available associations, with few of the problems of the Greek system, I now believe that choosing a sorority or fraternity above these others can be limiting, and even harmful, to students.

Of course, even with all its flaws, no one can deny that much good can come out of the Greek system. Fraternities and sororities offer leadership development, service learning, scholarship incentives, and a large network for cultivating lifelong friendships. My own experience certainly provided these benefits, especially the friendships. I met my husband through the Greek system, and made many friends with whom I am still very close. But considering the many problems in its current structure, I have to say that even the benefit of forming lasting friendships is not enough to justify joining the Greek system.

The Greek system also provides students with helpful business connections. Many of its members have become successful leaders in our society. More than fifty fraternity men have served as U.S. Supreme Court Justices; fifteen have been president of the U.S. Supreme Court Justices; and fifteen have served as president of the United States, including John F. Kennedy, Ronald

Reagan, and George Bush. Other alumni include entertainers such as Bob Hope, Candice Bergen, Dionne Warwick, Tom Selleck, and Joanne Woodward; heads of Fortune 500 companies, such as Sam Walton; and other prominent individuals such as Winnie Mandela, Lou Gehrig, and William Faulkner.[1]

However, I believe this impressive list only accentuates the great need to examine the issues in this book and bring about change. The Greek system has such power to influence the young, inexperienced, intelligent adults who choose to join, individuals who may be tomorrow's leaders. Thus, we should feel all the more compelled to get back to the humanitarian values its founders intended rather than the elite "party animalism" frequently promoted today.

The Greek system was initially intended to be an intellectual, rather than social, group. In the seventeenth century, the first fraternity was founded to discuss moral, philosophical, and other intellectual issues without being influenced by faculty. By the eighteenth century, Greek groups had become very popular. They met to hold debates of current events and other topics. For members, it was a form of relief from days spent in prayer and memorizing ancient languages and philosophies.

Soon, college became more accessible to increasing numbers of students with a broad range of interests. With the introduction of Greek houses in the middle of the nineteenth century, the role and prestige of fraternities gradually evolved from groups that met together to groups that lived together. By the 1880s, Greeks became known as an elite social group, and the intellectual reputation of the Greek system had all but disappeared.[2]

Today, it remains a predominantly social group. Over the years, however, Greek fraternities and sororities have become known for questionable and abusive behavior and values. Now, the need for reform has become so great that if something doesn't change, the system itself may collapse. As one researcher said, "Greeks have long held a special place in campus life. But without a concerted renewal effort indicating that fraternities and sororities can adapt to the changing campus environment, that place may soon be forfeited."[3]

Some institutions have already chosen to heed the many concerns about the Greek system, and have decided to ban certain problem groups.[4] For example, Duke University recently booted from campus a fraternity with a reputation for hard drinking and rowdiness.[5] Several small, private, liberal arts colleges—namely, Colby, Middlebury, and Amherst—have eliminated fraternities on their campuses altogether, as have other prestigious colleges such as Bucknell, Franklin and Marshall, and Williams.[6]

At Colgate University in Hamilton, New York, where fraternities have been an issue for the last ten years, more than five hundred students and staff staged a protest in 1994 against them; the faculty subsequently voted to abolish the system.

"[The Greek system] is detrimental to humane learning in a very broad sense," said Colgate's Ann Lane, who lobbied for change. "It's anti-intellectual in its core. Fraternities foster values that are in opposition to values we all uphold and respect."[7]

As James C. Arnold and George D. Kuh concluded in *Brotherhood and the Bottle: A Cultural Analysis of the Role of Alcohol in Fraternities,* "at least some, and perhaps many, fraternities need systematic cultural reform to become minimally congruent with the educational aims of their institution and more consistently attain the noble goals to which they aspire."

Indeed, students would have much to gain if the Greek system returned to its original principles of upholding brotherhood and sisterhood, the ideas of others, and valuable spiritual and academic goals. By returning to these ideals, the organization could once again function as a safe environment, providing a caring and supportive environment where students could learn, improve communication and leadership skills, and encounter the responsibilities and joys of giving.

The National Interfraternity Conference, the National Panhellenic Conference, Greek councils, National Pan'Hellenic Councils, writers, and researchers have made specific suggestions for fraternities and sororities to help bring reform, but few organizations have volunteered to institute major changes. Of those who have, most have done so in an attempt to minimize negative exposure. Leaders of fraternities and sororities seem to be distracted from bringing the needed change, being too often concerned with liability issues, the need to avoid prosecution, and the desire to change behavior of individual chapter members.

The fact that external forces such as university officials are beginning to force these changes in the Greek system suggests that Greeks might be unable to live out what they profess to believe, which means they are no longer fulfilling their traditional purposes. Colleges and universities around the nation show that Greek organizations continually receive requests to reform, but they remain opposed. It may be that vital improvement cannot be attained—but without it, the system may need to be shut down.

I expect that some people with ties to the Greek system will disagree with a number of the perceptions, explanations, and conclusions presented herein. I realize that there may be campuses whose organizations provide a more healthy environment, and if so, I applaud them. Yet, my purpose for writing this book remains: students and parents need to be aware of these major flaws in the Greek system, before they decide to participate. My desire is that this book will stimulate the discussion and critical debate needed once again to see the Greek system as a productive and educational force in the next decade and beyond.

The final decision rests with the colleges and universities that permit fraternities and sororities to operate on their campuses. And if individual houses are unwilling to conduct themselves in a respectable, positive manner, these colleges and universities should take responsibility for their students by demanding reform. Parents trust these schools to provide a positive experience for their sons and daughters; at the very least, college administrators owe them that.

ΠΔΣΩΠΔΣΩΠΔΣΩΠΔΣΩΠΔΣΩΠΔΣ

NOTES

CHAPTER 1—HAZING

1. Kelly T. Yee, "Fraternity, Sorority Hazing Under Increased Scrutiny," *New Orleans Times-Picayune,* 11 September 1994, sec. A, p. 12.

2. Irving L. Janis, *Victims of Groupthink: A Psychological Study of Foreign-Policy Decisions and Fiascoes* (Boston: Houghton Millflin Company, 1972), 5.

3. Hank Nuwer, *Broken Pledges: The Deadly Rite of Hazing* (Atlanta: Longstreet Press, 1990), 115.

4. Ibid.

5. Gordon Atlas and Dean Morier, "The Sorority Rush Process: Self-Selection, Acceptance Criteria, and the Effect of Rejection," *Journal of College Student Development* 35 (September 1994): 346.

6. Nuwer, *Broken Pledges,* 115.

7. David Mills, "Fraternity Violence: The Pledging Debate," *Los Angeles Times,* 24 July 1990, sec. E, pg. 8.

8. H. Witt, "Breaking the Pledges: A Mind Is a Terrible Thing to Waste," *Chicago Tribune,* 23 May 1983, sec. A, pg. 13.

9. Andrew Merton, "Random Mayhem" and "Return to Brotherhood," *Ms.,* September/October 1985, 60–65, 122.

10. Douglas R. Richmond, "The Legal Implications of Fraternity Hazing," *NASPA Journal* 26, no. 4 (Summer 1989): 300.

11. Associated Press, "Bastrop (Texas) Authorities Investigating Tips That Student Died in Hazing," *The Dallas Morning News*, 4 May 1995, sec. D, pg. 12.

12. "Hazing Ends in Death," *Cincinnati Post*, 17 February 1994, sec. A, pg. 2.

13. Yee, "Hazing under Scrutiny," sec. A, p. 12.

14. Nuwer, *Broken Pledges*, 120.

15. Ibid.

16. Ibid.

17. John L. Bair and Patrick S. Williams, "Fraternity Hazing Revisited: Current Alumni and Active Member Attitudes Toward Hazing," *Journal of College Students Personnel* 24, no. 4 (1983): 300–305.

18. Adam Weintraub, "Three More People Say Hazing Occurred at M.U. Fraternity," *Cincinnati Enquirer*, 21 April 1994, sec. B, pg. 1.

CHAPTER 2—SEXISM AND SEXUAL HARASSMENT

1. Robin Warshaw, *I Never Called It Rape* (New York: Harper & Row, 1988), 105.

2. Mindy Stombler, "'Buddies' or 'Slutties': The Collective Sexual Reputation of Fraternity Little Sisters," *Gender & Society* 8, no. 3 (September 1994): 303.

3. Kathleen Hirsch, "Fraternities of Fear: Gang Rape, Male Bonding, and the Silencing of Women," *Ms.*, September/October 1990, 54.

4. J. Hughes and B. Sandler, *Peer Harassment: Hassles for Women on Campus* (Washington, D.C.: Association of American Colleges, Project on the Status and Education of Women, 1988), 29.

5. Linda Kalof and Timothy Cargill, "Fraternity and Sorority Membership and Gender Dominance Attitudes," *Sex Roles* 25, no. 7/8 (1991): 417–23.

6. Patricia Yancey Martin and Robert A. Hummer, "Fraternities and Rape on Campus," *Gender & Society* 3, no. 4 (December 1989): 466.

7. Jan Miller, "Little Sisters, What's the Problem?" *The Future* (Winter 1988–89), 23.

8. Stombler, "'Buddies' or 'Slutties,'" 308.

9. Warshaw, *I Never Called It Rape,* 107–8.

10. Stombler, "'Buddies' or 'Slutties,'" 308.

11. Fred Yoder, "Little Sisters—A Privilege or a Problem?" *Sigma Chi National Magazine* (Spring 1989): 1.

12. Nick McKay, "Description of Events," *U.S.C. Derby Days Magazine* (Spring 1990), 1.

13. Ibid.

14. Kalof and Cargill, "Fraternity and Sorority Membership," 417–423.

15. Martin and Hummer, "Fraternities and Rape on Campus," 462.

16. Andrew Merton, "Return to Brotherhood: An Exposé of Fraternity Life Today," *Ms.,* September/October 1985, 60–65

17. A. Garry, "Pornography and Respect for Women," in R. Baker and F. Elliston (eds.) *Philosophy and Sex,* rev. ed. (Buffalo, N.Y.: Prometheus books, 1984), 312–26.

18. Ibid.

19. Susan Tifft, "Waging War on the Greeks," *Time,* 16 April 1990, 64.

20. Ibid, 65.

21. Ibid.

CHAPTER 3—RAPE

1. Peggy Reeves Sanday, *Fraternity Gang Rape: Sex, Brotherhood, and Privilege on Campus (*New York: New York University Press, 1990).

2. Kathleen Hirsch, "Fraternities of Fear: Gang Rape, Male Bonding, and the Silencing of Women," *Ms.,* September/October 1990, 52.

3. Stacey Copenhaver and Elizabeth Grauerholz, "Sexual Victimization among Sorority Women: Exploring the Link Between Sexual Violence and Institutional Practices," *Sex Roles* 24 (1991): 38.

4. Hirsch, "Fraternities of Fear," 52.

5. *The Record* (Spring 1990): 15.

6. Patricia Yancey Martin and Robert A. Hummer, "Fraternities and Rape on Campus," *Gender & Society* 3, no. 4 (December 1989): 458.

7. Julie K. Ehrhart and Bernice R. Sandler, *Campus Gang Rape: Party Games?* (Washington, D.C.: Association of American Colleges, 1985).

8. M. E. O'Shaughnessey and C. J. Palmer, Summary report, ERIC Document Reproduction Service, no. ED 267667, University of Illinois, Champaign, 1990.

9. M. P. Koss and T. E. Dinero, "Discriminant Analysis of Risk Factors for Sexual Victimization among a National Sample of College Women," *Journal of Consulting and Clinical Psychology* (1989): 242–50.

10. Copenhaver and Grauerholz, "Sexual Victimization," 37.

11. Vickie Bane, "Silent No More," *People,* 17 December 1990, 94.

12. Ibid.

13. Hirsch, "Fraternities of Fear," 52–53.

14. Copenhaver and Grauerholz, "Sexual Victimization," 36–40.

15. Martin and Hummer, "Fraternities and Rape," 458–459.

16. Copenhaver and Grauerholz, "Sexual Victimization," 39.

17. Ibid, 39–40.

18. Denise M. Worth, Pamela A. Matthews, and Warren R. Coleman, "Sex Role, Group Affiliation, Family Background, and Courtship Violence in College Students," *Journal of College Student Development* 31 (May 1990): 251–52.

19. Copenhaver and Grauerholz, "Sexual Victimization," 37.

20. Michele N. K. Collison, "Although Fraternities Bear Brunt of Criticism for Hazing, Activities of Sororities, Too, Stir Concerns on Campuses," *The Chronicle of Higher Education* A (10 October 1990): 40.

21. Hirsch, "Fraternities of Fear," 55.

22. Copenhaver and Grauerholz, "Sexual Victimization," 31–41.

23. J. Garrett-Gooding and R. Senter, Jr., "Attitudes and Acts of Sexual Aggression on a University Campus," *Sociological Inquiry,* no. 57 (1987): 348–71.

24. N.M. Malamuth and J.V.P. Check, "The Effects of Aggressive Pornography on Beliefs in Rape Myths: Individual Differences," *Journal of Research in Personality* 19 (1985), 261.

25. Hirsch, "Fraternities of Fear," 54–55.

26. Constance Johnson, "When Sex Is the Issue," *U.S. News and World Report,* 7 October 1990, 36.

27. Ibid.

28. Hirsch, "Fraternities of Fear," 55.

CHAPTER 4—DRUGS AND ALCOHOL

1. James C. Arnold and George D. Kuh, *Brotherhood and the Bottle: A Cultural Analysis of the Role of Alcohol in Fraternities* (Bloomington, Ind.: Center for the Study of the College Fraternity, 1992), 1.

2. Sigma Alpha Epsilon, "Sobering Lessons on Campus," *The Record* (7 December 1994), 1.

3. Scott Martelle, "Why Co-Eds Drink," *Detroit News,* 14 June 1994, 14.

4. "Sobering Lessons," 1.

5. H. Wechler and N. Isaac, "'Binge' Drinkers at Massachusetts Colleges: Prevalence, Drinking, Style, Time Trends, and Associated Problems," *JAMA* 267, no. 21 (1992): 2929–31.

6. "Sobering Lessons," 1.

7. U.S. Department of Health and Human Services, *Drug Use among American High School Seniors, College Students, and Young Adults, 1975–1990; II: College Students and Young Adults,* by L. D. Johnston, P. M. O'Malley, and J. G. Bachman (Washington, D.C.: 1991).

8. "Sobering Lessons," 1.

9. Scott Martelle, "Why Co-Eds Drink," 14.

10. Leonard Goodwin, "Alcohol and Drug Use in Fraternities and Sororities," *Journal of Alcohol and Drug Education* 37, no. 2 (Winter 1992): 61.

11. Dale R. Tampke, "Alcohol Behavior, Risk Perception, and Fraternity and Sorority Membership," *NASPA Journal* 28, no. 1 (Fall 1990): 72.

12. Hugh Klein, "College Students' Attitudes toward the Use of Alcoholic Beverages," *Journal of Alcohol and Drug Education* 37, no. 3 (1992): 35–52.

13. George D. Kuh and James C. Arnold, "Liquid Bonding: A Cultural Analysis of the Role of Alcohol in Fraternity Pledgeship," *Journal of College Student Development* 34 (September 1993): 329.

14. Leonard Goodwin, "Explaining Alcohol Consumption and Related Experiences among Fraternity and Sorority Members," *Journal of College Student Development* 30 (September 1989): 448.

15. Arnold and Kuh, *Brotherhood and the Bottle,* 24–25.

16. Robin Warshaw, "In the Bonds of Fraternity," *The Nation,* August 21–28, 1989, 207–8.

17. David Grogan, Bill Shaw, Ron Ridenhour, Andrea Fine, and Maria Eftimiades, "Their Brothers' Keepers?" *People,* 24 May 1993, 65–66.

18. "Sobering Lessons," 1.

19. Allie Shah, "Why Do 'U' Students Use More Tobacco, Drugs?" *Minneapolis/St. Paul Star Tribune,* 28 December 1994, sec. B, p. 1.

20. Joe Treen, "When Cops Came to Fraternity Row," *People,* 1 July 1991, 28–31.

21. Pamela Manson, "Minors' Drinking Can Snare Host," *Arizona Republic,* 14 July 1994, sec. B, p. 1.

22. John Chandler, "CSUN Fraternity Appeals Sanctions," *Los Angeles Times,* 11 March 1995, sec. B, p. 2.

23. "Police Raid Wisconsin Fraternity Party," The Associated Press, downloaded from America Online News Service (April 28, 1995).

24. "Sobering Lessons," 1.

CHAPTER 5—RISKY SEX

1. Shari Roan, "Sexually Transmitted Diseases Flourishing," *Sacramento Bee,* 9 November 1994, sec. A, p. 5.

2. "Condom Shock: The Threat of Pregnancy," *Glamour,* May 1995, 211.

3. Danny R. Hoyt and Les B. Whitbeck, "Campus Prestige and Dating Behaviors," *College Student Journal* 25, no. 4 (December 1991): 460.

4. Sally K. Ward and Susan Ault, "Fraternity and Sorority Membership, AIDS Knowledge and Safe-Sex Practices," *Sociology and Social Research* 74, no. 3 (April 1990): 159.

5. EPM Communications, Inc., "Sex and the College Student," *Research Alert* 12, no. 17 (2 September 1994): 1.

6. Dr. Richard Keeling, *Health Watch,* " NBC Nightly News," 11 April 1995.

7. Charles B. Clayman, M.D., *The American Medical Association Family Medical Guide* (New York: Random House, 1994), 657.

8. Helene D. Gayle, Richard P. Keeling, Miguel Garcia-Tunon, Barbara W. Kilbourne, John P. Narkunas, Fred R. Ingram, Martha F. Rogers, and James W. Curran, "Prevalence of the Human Immunodeficiency Virus among University Students," *The New England Journal of Medicine* 323, no. 22 (29 November 1990): 1540.

9. Roan, "Diseases Flourishing," sec. A, p. 5.

10. Dr. (Gifford-)Jones, (Q78) "Sex and Myths: Sexually Transmitted Diseases Are Tougher Than You Think," *Montreal Gazette*, 6 March 1994, sec. C, p. 5.

11. Clayman, *Family Medical Guide*, 656.

12. Gifford-Jones, "Sex and Myths," sec. C, p. 5.

13. Ward and Ault, "AIDS Knowledge," 159.

14. Ibid.

15. Edward M. Mink, Linda Mareth, Jo Russell, and Michael Young, "Correlates of Condom Use among Fraternity Men," *Psychological Reports* 68 (1991): 256–57.

16. Les Parrott, III, *Helping the Struggling Adolescent* (Grand Rapids, Mich.: Zondervan Publishing House, 1993), 243

CHAPTER 6—RUSH AND PLEDGING

1. Gordon Atlas and Dean Morier, "The Sorority Rush Process: Self-Selection, Acceptance Criteria, and the Effect of Rejection," *Journal of College Student Development* 35 (September 1994): 351.

2. Susan Mongell and Alvin E. Roth, "Sorority Rush As a Two-Sided Matching Mechanism," *The American Economic Review* 81, no. 3 (June 1991): 441.

3. Ibid, 443.

4. Robert Ackerman, "The Survival of Greek Life: Concerns and Solutions," *NASPA Journal* 28, no. 1 (Fall 1990), 78.

5. Mongell and Roth, "Two-Sided Matching Mechanism," 447.

6. Ibid, 443.

7. Ibid, 451–53.

8. Atlas and Morier, "Sorority Rush Process," 346, 352.

9. Michael J. Keller and Derrell Hart, "The Effects of Sorority and Fraternity Rush on Students' Self-Images," *Journal of College Student Personnel* (May 1982): 257–58.

10. Richard G. Bowker, "Correlates of Pledging and

Academic Performance in an Introductory Biology Course," *NASPA Journal* 31, no. 4 (summer 1994): 264.

CHAPTER 7—THE PERFECT GREEK IMAGE

1. Jeanette N. Cleveland, "Using Hypothetical and Actual Applicants in Assessing Person-Organization Fit: A Methodological Note," *Journal of Applied Social Psychology* 12 (1991): 1010.

2. Linda Louise Boynton-Arthur, Ph.D., *Idealized Images: Appearances and the Construction of Femininities in Two Exclusive Organizations* (Davis: University of California, 1992), 262.

3. Boynton-Arthur, *Idealized Images,* 262.

4. Christian S. Crandall, "Social Contagion of Binge Eating," *Journal of Personality and Social Psychology* 55, no. 4 (1988): 588.

5. Chris Kaltenbach, "Drawing the Line," *Baltimore Sun,* 21 February 1995, sec. D, pg. 1.

6. Joan Kelly Bernard, "Doubts, Questions Precede Plastic Surgery," *Arizona Republic,* 15 November 1994, sec. E, pg. 1.

7. Ibid.

8. Thomas L. Flannery, "Steroids Aren't New; But Dangers Remain," *Lancaster (Penn.) Intelligencer Journal,* 14 July 1994, sec. A, pg. 7.

9. James Deacon, "Biceps in a Bottle: Teenagers Turn to Steroids to Build Muscles," *Maclean's,* 2 May 1994, 52.

10. Flannery, "Steroids Aren't New," sec. A, pg. 7.

11. Ibid.

12. Deacon, "Biceps in a Bottle," 52.

13. Charles E. Yesalis, Nancy J. Kennedy, Andrea N. Kopstein, and Michael S. Bahrke, "Anabolic-androgenic Steroid Use in the United States," *Journal of American Medical Association* 270, no. 10 (8 September 1993): 1217.

14. Anne McElroy, *The Kappa Alpha Theta Magazine* 108, no. 3 (Spring 1994): 5.

15. Crandall, "Social Contagion," 588.

16. Philip W. Meilman, Ph.D., Frank A. Von Hippel, and Michael S. Gaylor, M.D., "Self-Induced Vomiting in College Women: Its Relation to Eating, Alcohol Use, and Greek Life," *JACH* 40 (July 1991): 40.

17. Crandall, "Social Contagion," 588.

18. Michele Siegel, Ph.D., Judith Brisman, Ph.D., and Margot Weinshel, M.S.W., *Surviving an Eating Disorder: Strategies for Family and Friends* (New York: Harper & Row, 1988): 27.

19. A. J. Carr, "Courtly Return to Victory over Losing," *Raleigh (N.C.) News & Observer,* 8 October 1994, sec. C, pg. 1.

CHAPTER 8—RIVALRY

1. Kathy Loan, "Five Radford Fraternity Members Charged," *Roanoke (Va.) Times & World News,* 17 March 1994, sec. C, pg. 3.

2. "University of Nebraska-Kearney Fraternity Party Nets Arrest of Four Men," *Omaha World Herald,* 10 April 1994, sec. B, pg. 7.

3. Patricia Yancey Martin and Robert A. Hummer, "Fraternities and Rape on Campus," *Gender & Society* 3, no. 4 (December 1989): 466.

CHAPTER 9—RACISM

1. Stephen Schmitz and Sean Alan Forbes, "Choices in a No-Choice System: Motives and Biases in Sorority Segregation," *Journal of College Development* 35 (March 1994): 103.

2. W. A. Bryan, "Contemporary Fraternity and Sorority Issues," *New Directions for Student Services,* no. 40 (1987): 47.

3. Schmitz and Forbes, "Choices in a No-Choice System," 103.

4. Edward G. Whipple, John L. Baier, and David L. Grady, "a Comparison of Black and White Greeks at a Predominantly

White University," *NASPA Journal* 28, no. 2 (Winter 1991): 140–41.

5. A. Press, "Fraternities Under Fire," *Newsweek on Campus,* April 1988, 8.

6. Andrew Merton, "Return to Brotherhood: An Exposé of Fraternity Life Today," *Ms.,* September/October 1985, 65.

7. Press, "Fraternities Under Fire," 10.

8. David Grogan, Bill Shaw, Ron Ridenhour, Andrea Fine, and Maria Eftimiades, "Their Brothers' Keepers?" *People* 24 May 1993, 68.

9. "Fraternity Skit Ruled Constitutional: George Mason University Contest Called Racist and Sexist," *Washington Post,* 12 May 1993, sec. D, pg. 5.

10. Kelly Garbus, "Medieval Costumes Seen as Racial Insult," *Kansas City (Mo.) Star,* 22 April 1995, sec. C, pg. 1.

11. Larry Gordon, "Fraternity Faces Sanctions for Offensive Songbook," *Los Angeles Times,* 2 October 1992, sec. B, pg. 1.

12. Drew Williams, "I.S.U. Student Arrested in Fraternity Brawl," *Peoria (Ill.) Journal Star,* 7 December 1994, sec. B, pg. 8.

13. "White Fraternity In Memphis Shut Down after Racial Incident Led Up to Interracial Brawl," *Jet* 88, no. 22 (9 October 1995): 23.

14. "University of Arkansas Suspends White Frat That Had 'Sambo' Statue and Whose Members Threw Chair at Black Professor," *Jet* 88, no. 22 (9 October 1995): 22.

15. Schmitz and Forbes, "Choices in a No-Choice System," 106.

16. Kathleen Kelleher, "A Pledge to Bring Diversity to Frat Row," *Los Angeles Times,* 28 April 1991, sec. E, pg. 7.

17. Susan Tifft, "Waging War on the Greeks," *Time,* 16 April 1990, 65.

18. Schmitz and Forbes, "Choices in a No-Choice System," 103, 105.

19. Ibid, 106.

20. Ibid, 104–105.

21. Ibid, 107.

22. A. D. Gadson, "Greek Power! African-American Greek Letter Organizations Yield Massive Influence after School Days," *Black Collegian* (September/October 1989): 36.

23. Whipple, Baier, and Grady, "Comparison of Black and White Greeks," 146.

24. Gadson, "Greek Power!" 36.

25. Whipple, Baier, and Grady, "Comparison of Black and White Greeks," 146.

AFTERWORD

1. James C. Arnold and George D. Kuh, *Brotherhood and the Bottle: A Cultural Analysis of the Role of Alcohol in Fraternities* (Bloomington, Ind.: Center for the Study of the College Fraternity, 1992), 84.

2. Ibid., 111.

3. Robert Ackerman, "The Survival of Greek Life: Concerns and Solutions," *NASPA Journal* 28, no. 1 (Fall 1990): 81.

4. Susan Tifft, "Waging War on the Greeks," *Time,* 16 April 1990, 64.

5. Catherine Clabby, "Fraternity Dissolved by Duke," *Raleigh (N.C.) News & Observer,* 17 March 1994, sec. B, pg. 1.

6. Alan D. Miller, "Denison May Try to Close Fraternity Houses," *The Columbus (Ohio) Dispatch,* 20 November 1994, sec. B, pg. 1.

7. Kathleen Hirsch, "Fraternities of Fear: Gang Rape, Male Bonding, and the Silencing of Women," *Ms.* September/October 1990, 52.

ΠΔΣΩΠΔΣΩΠΔΣΩΠΔΣΩΠΔΣΩΠΔΣ

GLOSSARY

Active: a member who is actively involved with his or her fraternity or sorority.

Affiliate: a fraternity or sorority member who has transferred from another college and wants to continue membership in the same Greek chapter at their new college.

Alumni: a graduate and former student of a specific school, university or college.

Bid: an invitation that asks rushees to become pledges of a fraternity or a sorority.

Big Brother: an active fraternity member who is assigned to befriend a new fraternity pledge or little sister pledge.

Big Sister: an active sorority member who is assigned to befriend a new sorority pledge.

Chapter: a membership system of a national or international sorority or fraternity.

College Panhellenic Association: the combining campus organization of college members of National Panhellenic Conference sororities.

De-pledged: when a fraternity or sorority pledge can no longer remain a pledge.

Exchanges: parties, usually with a theme, between fraternities and sororities.

Fraternity: a Greek-letter men's organization (sometimes a women's organization).

Greeks: those who belong to a college fraternity or sorority.

Greek Advisor: a designated person or persons, usually one assigned per campus, who serves as an advisor to fraternity and sorority members.

Greek System: an assemblage of college Greek fraternity and sorority organizations.

Hazing: an initiation custom meant deliberately to cause mental or physical displeasure, embarrassment, harassment, or mockery.

Hell Master: a member of a fraternity or sorority who is appointed to terrorize the pledges during Hell Week.

Hell Week: a designated week devoted to hazing pledges.

House: a place that houses fraternity or sorority members.

House Director: a resident adult employed at the fraternity or sorority to manage the house.

Inactive: an initiated fraternity or sorority member who decides not to participate as a member.

Initiation: a ritualistic ceremony that pledges must go through to gain membership into a fraternity or a sorority

Interfraternity Council (IFC): the combining campus organization of college members belonging to the National Interfraternity Conference.

Legacy: sorority or fraternity members whose parents, siblings, or grandparents were in the same sorority or fraternity.

Little Sisters: a selected group of women who affiliate and support a fraternity.

Member: an individual who belongs to a fraternity or sorority.

National Interfraternity Conference (NIC): an organization created for college Greek social fraternities to support and cooperate with colleges and universities in pursuing high academic and social regulations.

National Panhellenic Conference (NPC): an organization created for college Greek social sororities to support and cooperate with colleges and universities in pursuing high academic and social regulations.

National Pan'Hellenic Council (NPHC): an organization consisting of eight African-American sororities and fraternities.

Neophyte: a pledge that did not meet the requirements of becoming a member but is allowed another chance to meet the requirements.

Pledge: a student who is trying to make the requirements to become a member of a fraternity or a sorority.

Pledge Order: the order in which pledges line up (often by height).

Preference: the last two rush parties.

Preferential Bidding: the system used during rush that matches rushee and sorority preferences.

Released: those who had a parent, sibling, or grandparent in a sorority or fraternity.

Rush: a structured period when fraternities and sororities select new pledges.

Rush Chairman: the fraternity or sorority member who is responsible for planning rush for their house.

GLOSSARY

Rushee: a college student who is interested in being selected to become a fraternity or sorority pledge.

Silence: the time period during rush when a pledge is not allowed to communicate with active Greek members.

Social Chairman: the fraternity or sorority member who is responsible for planning the social events for their house.

Sorority: a Greek letter women's organization.

Star: a pledge who has all of the qualities desired of a new member.

ΠΔΣΩΠΔΣΩΠΔΣΩΠΔΣΩΠΔΣΩΠΔΣ

RESOURCES

Each of these organizations provides numerous services and resources. They offer information through conferences, counseling, videos, printed materials, and more.

AIDS Information Ministries
6032 Jacksboro Hwy., Ste. 100
Lake Worth, TX 76135
Duane Crumb, President
(817) 237-3146

AIDS Task Force for the American College Health Association
c/o Dr. Richard P. Keeling, University Health Services
University of Wisconsin-Madison
1552 University Ave.
Madison, WI 53705
(608) 262-1234

Alcohol Research Information Services
1106 E. Oakland, Lansing MI 48906
Robert Hammond, Executive Director
(517) 485-9900
Publishes information on alcohol related topics.

Alternatives to Fear
1605 17th Ave.
Seattle, WA 98122
(206) 344-4827
Provides education on acquaintance rape and defense classes.

American Council for Drug Education
136 E. 64th St.
New York NY 10021
(212) 977-3354

American Council on Alcoholism
2522 St. Paul St.
Baltimore, MD 21218
Robert G. Kirk, Executive Director
(410) 889-0100
Provides information, short term counseling and referrals to recommended alcoholic treatment centers.

American Council on Alcohol Problems
3426 Bridgeland Dr.
Bridelton, MO 63044
Dr. Curt Scarborough, Executive Director
(314) 739-5944
Supplies individuals with information relating to alcohol problems.

American Outreach Association
PO Box 25042, Colorado Springs, CO 80936
Charles Prusch, Director
(719) 592-1134

American School Counselor Association
5999 Stevenson Ave.
Alexandria, VA 22304-3300
Scott R. Swirling, Executive Director
(703) 823-9800
Covers a broad range of topics that concern college students.

Association of Fraternity Advisors
3901 W. 86th St., Ste. 390
Indianapolis, IN 46268
Michael Hayes, President
(317) 876-4691

Association for University and College Counseling Center
Directors, c/o Herbert Horikawa,
Temple University Counseling Center
Sulevan Hall (007-085),
Philadelphia, PA 19122
(215) 787-7276

The Bacchus and Gamma Peer Education Network
P.O. Box 100430
Denver, CO 80250-0430
(303) 871- 3068

Cambridge Documentary
P.O. Box 385
Cambridge, MA 02139
(617)354-3677
Offers *Calling the Shots*—a video on the tactics used in advertising to promote alcohol.

Central Productions, Inc.
3111 Broadway
San Antonio, TX 78203
(210) 828-6098; (800) 251-7867
Offers *Trust Your Instincts*—a video that shows you how using your instincts can give you an edge when threatened or attacked.

C.H.U.C.K. (Committee to Halt Useless College Killings)
P.O. Box 188
Sayville NY 11782
Eileen Stevens, President
(516) 567-1130

Citizens for a Drug Free America
3595 Bayside Walk
San Diego CA 92109-7451
Roger Chapin, President
(707) 207-9300

Chimera
59 E. Van Buren Ave., #714
Chicago, IL 60605
Offers self defense programs

Committees of Correspondence
24 Adams Street
Danvers, MA 01923-2718
Otto Moulton, President
(508) 774-2641

Coronet/ MTI Film and Video
108 Wilmot Rd.
Deerfield, IL 60015
Provides videos on campus acquaintance rape.

Gamma Peer Management Network
PO Box 100430
Denver, CO 80250
Drew Hunter, Executive Director
(303) 871-3068

The Health Connection
55 W. Oak Ridge Dr.
Hagerstown, MD 21740
Robert Kinney, President
(301) 790-9735

International Society for AIDS Education and Prevention
341 Poncedeleon Ave.
Atlanta, Go 30308
(404) 616-97991

National Academic Advising Association
Kansas State Univ.
2323 Anderson Ave., Ste. 225
Manhattan, KS 66502,
Robert Flaherty, Executive Director
(913) 532-5717

National Association of Alcohol and Drug Abuse Counselors
3717 Columbia Pike, Ste. 300
Arlington, VA 22204-4254
Linda Kaplan, Executive Director
(703) 920-4644

National Association of University Women
c/o Phyllis Eggleston, President
1501 11th St. NW
Washington, DC 20001
(202) 547-3967

National Clearinghouse on Marital and Date Rape
2325 Oak St.
Berkeley CA 94708
Laura X, Director
(510) 524-1582

National Coalition against Sexual Assault
912 N. 2nd St.
Harrisburg, PA 17102
Katie Issari, President
(202) 483-7165

National Coalition for Women and Girls in Education
c/o Girl Scouts of the USA
1025 Connecticut Ave. NW, Ste.309
Washington, DC 20036
Carmen Delgado Votaw, Chair
(202) 659-3780

National Council on Alcoholism and Drug Dependence
12 W. 21st St.
New York NY 10010
Paul Wood Ph. D., President
(212) 206-6770

National Interfraternity Conference
3901 West 86th Street Suite 390
Indianapolis, IN 46268
Jonathan Brant, Executive Vice President
(317) 872-1112
Provides numerous resources and services to member fraternities
and college campuses.

National Identification Program for the Advancement of Women
in Higher Education Administration
Office of Women in Higher Education
1 Dupont Cir. NW
Washington, DC 20036
Donna Shavik, Director
(202) 939-9390

National Pan'Hellenic Council
Memorial Hall W. 108
Bloomington, IN 47405
(812) 855-8820
Stresses and provides action strategies on matters of mutual concern for their eight African American fraternities and sororities

National Prevention Network
444 N. Capitol St. NW, Ste. 642
Washington, DC 20001
Stephanie Kashangki, President
(202) 783-6868

National Panhellenic Conference
3901 West 86th Street Suite 380
Indianapolis, IN 46268
(317) 872-3185
Provides numerous services and resources to member sororities
and college campuses.

National Women Student's Coalition
c/o USSA
815 15th St. NW
Washington, DC 20036
Stephanie Arellano, President
(202) 347-8772

Partnership for a Drug Free America
405 Lexington Ave.
New York, NY 10174
Richard Bonnette, President
(212) 922-1560

Rape Treatment Center
Santa Monica Hospital Medical Center
1250 Sixteenth Street
Santa Monica, CA 9404
Campus Rape Video available

The Society for the Advancement of Women's Health Research
1920 L. Street N.W., Suite 510
Washington, D.C. 20036
(202) 223-8224

TOVA—The Other Victims of Alcoholism
PO Box 1528, Radio City Station
New York, NY 10101
Josie Balaban Couture, President
(212) 247-8087

Unitarian Universalist Society for Alcohol and Drug Education
83 Sea St., PO Box 38
North Weymouth, MA 02191
Rev. Thomas Martin, Director
(617) 335-8504

Women Against Rape
Box 02084
Columbus, OH 43202
(614) 291-9751

Women's College Coalition
125 Michigan Ave. NE
Washington, DC 20017
Jadwiga S. Sebrechts, Director
(202) 234-0443

ΠΔΣΩΠΔΣΩΠΔΣΩΠΔΣΩΠΔΣΩΠΔΣ

INDEX